Advanced Praise for *Quarks of Light*

"As I started out to read *Quarks of Light*, I had an idea in my mind as to the type of spiritual or religious theme that may be shared in Mr. Gentile's story. Of course, that idea was based on my own religious/spiritual upbringing and belief system. What I found was not expected. Instead, it opened up my mind and heart to something greater, something that anyone can believe, regardless of their specific belief in a God or other knowledge of life now or life after death.

Quarks of Light provides a personal insight into the experiences of Mr. Gentile at various times of his life, as a young child, and each separate life-threatening health-related crisis.

As I read the various accounts and experiences, I was filled with such love for Maria and Melanie, Rob's daughter and wife, as well as the many doctors and health providers he encountered along his journey. I wept when he met Jay and came to know Molli.

In addition to the specifics of each experience, described in surrealistic detail, this story opens up a far greater understanding of how each of us is part of each other and how our lives, in life and after death, are entwined. It provides a deeper recognition and desire to open our hearts to the goodness around us, and to seek and share the love that permeates within our souls, regardless of our individual beliefs. We are one. We are each a part of the light."

–Deborah Mecham, Roy, Utah

"I don't have enough words to describe this book! I do, however, believe that this is exactly what the entire world needs to hear right very now. What an amazing journey, and proof that there is more to life than what we are currently focused on. We all have something to take away from his experience, the good and the bad. Everyone and everything is connected through God's perfect light. All of humanity needs to read this book, and then it can be saved."

–Yvette Chmelar, DuBois, Pennsylvania

"I've just finished *Quarks of Light.* If the emotional ups and many downhill/dark moments don't bring you to tears you are not human. God has blessed this man for a reason and gave him a job to do. Testify! Life has a purpose, love others, share it often."

–Steven Ethridge, North Carolina

"As an agnostic, I approached Quarks of Light with caution. Gentile's story of recovery and its redemption was impressive to me, and yet as I read it I lost two dear friends to untimely death, so it was difficult for me to completely credit God with its positive outcome. Nevertheless, I was impressed with the depth of detail and faith expressed, and the clarity of its prose. If there are such things as miracles, this book without doubt captures the course of one."

–David Andrew Westwood,
Author of *The Paisley Tree House*

"My emotions started bubbling up during the first few paragraphs. By the end, I had mascara running down my face, and couldn't breathe out for fear a flood would tidal out my nose! I was left with a feeling of EVERYTHING. Joy, sadness, euphoria, loss, excitement... thoughts of beginnings, endings, and the state of our species. And myself. This is a stunning book. I LOVE *Quarks of Light*."

–Grace Sharington, Austin, Texas

"While there have been many books written on the 'near-death,' or more accurately, actual death and returning experience, *Quarks of Light* far exceeds these in message and content. Wonders encountered on the other side, and the all-time question, 'What happens when we die?' is amazingly addressed in *Quarks of Light*, with stunning detail. The book voices the full story of watching the suffering of those we love, the pains of having a special needs child, and the damaging effects, and sometimes even the ultimate destruction, social media has caused our children. As finely tuned athletes, we fight through the continual physical, emotional, and spiritual pain... until we can't. *Quarks of Light* discusses this too, in the unique way of relationship we have with one another, and the intimacy offered to us by our Creator – 1 John 4:8 'Whoever does not love, does not know God, because God is love.'"

–Fred Callahan, Mooresville, North Carolina

"I once heard a story about the publishing giant Louise Hay, who was on stage welcoming an audience of thousands to a weekend-long spiritual, health, and wellness event sponsored by her company, Hayhouse Publishing. Ahead lay dozens of workshops, classes, lectures, and meditation sessions led by a wide variety of teachers, researchers, and authors. Louise surprised everyone by declaring that every one of the session leaders would actually be communicating the exact same thing. How could this be? Some sessions were about meditation, some about nutrition, some about energy medicine, some about music therapy, and so forth. Louise said that even though the instructors came from different media, had different life paths, different methods, and different approaches, that the attendees might look for the common message in every teacher's lecture.

Rob Gentile's astonishing, beautiful, and miraculous near-death experience story is very different from and yet somehow exactly the same as the stories of other 'NDEers' in the same manner as those Hay House workshops. The 'different-ness' opens me to the possibility that no matter who you are, where you come from, what your past experiences are; no matter how separated you've become from yourself or your source, miracles can – and do – happen to anyone.

And it is the sameness of his story to other 'NDEers' that confirms, also, that miracles truly do exist. The more I encounter the unique-yet-similar experiences of those with profound spiritual breakthroughs, the more that 'sameness' leads me to trust in life, in love, in the power of compassion and forgiveness. The more I see the miracles in my own life. The more I trust that we are spiritual beings first and physical humans, a distant second. The more I understand the 'oneness' that is referenced by spiritual teachers, but that I could never grasp. Because in one way or another, all near-death experiences seem to point to the same thing.

I am no researcher, just someone extremely interested in what is revealed to near-death experiencers and how those revelations change them forever. I've read hundreds of NDE accounts; and I strongly recommend *Quarks of Light*. It is with profound love that Rob bares himself, his story, his vulnerability. The twists and turns of his unfolding challenges, and the miracles that result, left me in awe of the power of love and surrender. And I realized the common message that Louise Hay urged her workshop attendees to become aware of, the thread that runs through all truth, all life, all stories. It is here in this book, too, waiting for you to discover! Indulge yourself in *Quarks of Lights* and perhaps it will jumpstart your own discovery of miracles.

–Michele Ziemann-DeVos, McHenry, Illinois

"I loved this book! Rob Gentile tells a compelling narrative of having a massive heart attack, then flatlining. He tells of the things he saw on the other side, including a visit from a relative who had taken his own life, with a message of hope. Of a doctor who, against all hope, refused to give up. In addition to his narrative of his visit to 'The Ethereal,' he also shares his experiences of returning to this life, and his thoughts and musings about it all, relying heavily upon his personal journal, recorded while these events were fresh. He was told he needed a heart transplant to survive, and indeed, he did receive a new heart, accompanied by a number of unlikely events along the way. While awaiting a heart to come available, he experienced a second visit to the ethereal, where more understanding was made available. He saw a network of lights covering the whole world, showing him how we are all interconnected. For more on this, you will have to read the book. Also, he gets a message of hope and love about his daughter, who has Rett Syndrome. During his recovery, and helped by his new heart, he has strong urgings to connect with the family of his donor. I found this part of his journey both heartwarming and heart-wrenching—in ways that lifted me up. In the end, we are all connected. Separation is an illusion. Each individual is important, and there is hope for all. All in all, a good read. I highly recommend it. 5 stars out of 5."

–Corey Anderson, Clinton, Utah

"This book delves into the existence of coincidences or no coincidences, free will, love, and miracles. A very compelling read. Decide if it coincides with your beliefs of the afterlife."

–Fred Russel, Pennsylvania

"This story impacted me at a visceral level…I have such a strong sense of identification with this journey or, perhaps better-said, the spirit of the journey, that a deep and powerful excitement overwhelms me. I know this sounds strange, if not totally nuts, but I feel the way I imagine someone would if they come round a bend and walk smack dab into a place, they have been yearning for yet dared not to dream existed. I am filled with gratitude and joy. What on earth is going on with me? Thank you eternally."

–Lark Elizabeth, Nags Head, North Carolina

"You will have people who believe it is fiction, but also those who know it is real. Some parts were beyond my knowledge but will read again and again to hopefully gain wisdom. I don't know what should be said in a review, but just know you need to follow through with publishing. Your life story touched me in ways, I could go on and on. THANK YOU for your bravery in telling it."

–Carol Lopez, Warren, Pennsylvania

"Wow, this book is amazing! There are so many points and subjects embedded, that just about everyone could pick out a couple of instances in their own life that match up exactly with what Rob experienced and went through. It expresses how our conversion is completely a gift of love from God. Rob's ability to share his innermost feelings during his highs and lows, and then connect them all back to God and to the Light; confirms that there are no coincidences. Once we start to cooperate with the quiet voices, we will start to experience great joy. We will be able to look back and see that the Voice/Light/God has always been with us. Rob's story is for those that have to face their innermost fears, and for those who love someone that has had a spiritual awakening, this book allows the complete understanding of the spiritual conversion and experience – and to those that know in the innermost self, that they (we) are here to complete a mission from God, to do His work, through His grace."

–Rey Gonzales, Houston, Texas

"Guided by the memories captured in a lifetime of journaling, *Quarks of Light* is an emotion-packed journey of a man struggling to understand his life to this point and what may lay ahead. Rob Gentile weaves his memories of his childhood and youth spent desperately searching for identity and meaning; the challenges he and his wife, Melanie, encounter raising their special needs daughter, Maria; and the devastation of facing a massive heart attack at age 56. With the hope of a meaningful recovery quickly dissolving before his eyes, he begins to question whether the potential outcomes justify the attempts at recovery. With life offering more questions than answers, Rob can't help but attempt to take more control of the world around him. Family, friends, co-workers, medical professionals, and even casual strangers ultimately help him piece together the understanding that surrendering control is his gateway to where greater knowledge is housed.

Regardless of your beliefs or life's path, you will find yourself often in the pages of this book. You may relive your experiences as a 'Melanie,' keeping it all together and putting on a brave face as a loved one struggles with medical issues. Pages later you may see yourself as an individual, friend, or parent of someone challenged every day to fit into a world that doesn't seem to understand. As a person of faith, you will look to the examples of 'Paul,' the 'Rev' and others, and seek opportunities to be generous in sharing your own path of spiritual enlightenment and to provide physical and emotional comfort when you can. You will find yourself wanting to be kinder and more welcoming to casual conversations. And, of course, you will see yourself as Rob, trying to make sense of the unexplained in your life.

While you will not find all your answers in this book, the discoveries that he shares will provide comfort and hope to anyone who reads it."

–Janis Hillis, El Paso, Texas

QUARKS OF LIGHT

A Near-Death Experience

What I Saw That Opened My Heart

Rob A. Gentile

IGNITE PRESS
Fresno, California

Published in the United States by Ignite Press.
ignitepress.us

ISBN: 978-1-953655-16-5 (Amazon Print)
ISBN: 978-1-953655-17-2 (IngramSpark) PAPERBACK
ISBN: 978-1-953655-18-9 (IngramSpark) HARDCOVER
ISBN: 978-1-953655-19-6 (E-book)

For bulk purchase and for booking, contact:

Rob A. Gentile
https://robagentile.com/contact/

Library of Congress Control Number: 2020922009

Cover design by Antonello Addipietro
Edited by Chris Karmiol
Interior design by Jetlaunch Layout Services

For Maria, who proved to me that God exists.

ACKNOWLEDGEMENTS

As with any journey, it's the people you meet along the way and the lessons they share that make life meaningful and rewarding. In the Ethereal I saw the power of a single act to spread light, and I wish to thank the many friends, acquaintances, and people that I have never personally met, who prayed and supported me. Please forgive me for not mentioning each of you by name, but know that without your collective contributions... I would not be here today.

For my wife, Melanie, who taught me that prayers are answered. The night I flatlined, she dropped to her knees on the hospital floor and cried out to God to save me. Your unwavering commitment to me and this book made all the difference.

My brothers and their families offered undying support that carried me through the most difficult periods of my journey to heart transplant. My brother in Christ, "The Rev," kept me anchored in spirit.

Thank you to the doctors mentioned by name in this book— you are true healers of body, mind, and spirit. The nurses and therapists who nurtured me back to health—you really do have superpowers. I offer deep appreciation to Dr. Jean-Ronal Corbier. I cannot imagine a world without your contributions to children with special needs, like my daughter, Maria.

Rhonda Lauritzen of Evalogue. Life, writing coach, and mentor—without your loving guidance this book would not have been written.

Special recognition to Michael Tang and the Tang Foundation.

TABLE OF CONTENTS

Foreword by Dr. Jean-Ronel Corbier, MD xvii

Preface. xxiii

Chapter 1: The Glowing Orb 1

Chapter 2: Code Blue 7

Chapter 3: Seeking a New Heart 23

Chapter 4: Selection Process 57

Chapter 5: Thumper. 79

Chapter 6: The Darkness 91

Chapter 7: Into the Ethereal 105

Chapter 8: It's Not Home Anymore. 115

Chapter 9: All One 153

Chapter 10: Gifts of Adversity. 171

Chapter 11: Spiritual Beings, Clay Vessels. 189

Chapter 12: Identity Crisis 211

Quarks of Light. 229

About the Author 241

FOREWORD

One morning in January 2016, I was at work in my clinic when I received a call from Melanie Gentile. It was not about her daughter, Maria, who has a neurodegenerative condition called Rett syndrome, which almost exclusively affects girls, causing neurological symptoms that begin at infancy. Among other things, the condition is associated with seizures, which can be difficult to control. I thought Melanie was calling me regarding a seizure Maria was having. I have been Maria's pediatric neurologist for many years and have treated her for her seizures which have included multiple trips to the hospital (including ER, hospitalization, and ICU admission). This call, however, was different. It was not about Maria, but, rather, Melanie's husband Rob,who was in the hospital fighting for his life.

Although Rob was not my patient, Melanie knew she could call me with this emergency and I would do what I could. She is a well-informed and knowledgeable pharmacist who has had the opportunity to work and collaborate with several of the country's leading physicians. As a conventionally trained and board-certified neurologist, I have endeavored to learn everything I could about the brain and neurological conditions. Although I have had the opportunity to do part of my neurology training at leading institutions, including Johns Hopkins and Mayo Clinic, among others, I have also looked for answers beyond traditional medicine, hence my connection with Melanie, who was on that same path. Together we have developed safe and natural treatment protocols to help children with special needs.

When Melanie explained what was going on, I could hardly believe it. Her husband Rob suffered a massive heart attack and was in a coma; it was very uncertain if he would make it. I had not known Rob to be sick previously, so this news shocked me. Melanie was understandably shaken up.

I rearranged my day to go to the hospital, where I did my best to encourage Melanie and Rob's brothers. I spoke to some of the ICU physicians who told me that Rob was in critical condition. Based on my neurology training and experience, I knew that Rob's prognosis and current clinical status were dire with the possibility of death, or at least severe cardiac and neurological sequelae. I told Melanie that it was in God's hands, and if it was His will then Rob would pull through—in my heart I knew that healing was possible.

As the days unfolded, doctors determined that Rob needed a cardiac transplantation, i.e., a new heart.

I later had the opportunity to see Rob in a hospital in Chicago prior to the heart transplantation. From the beginning, when Rob started telling me about his near-death experience, I immediately knew he needed to write a book, and after his surgery I encouraged him on several occasions to do so. It was clear to me that his story would touch many lives, as it had mine.

There is something in *Quarks of Light* for everyone. It covers spirituality, medicine, the philosophy of life, science, society, and more. While reading this book you may feel the urge to re-examine your life and make sure you are living to the fullest. You may look at others with more understanding, or ponder meditatively on the meaning of life and death. You may at times, as I have, laugh, cry, or express any number of emotions. Whether you are a parent of a child with special needs, a physician like me, a church leader, a chronically ill individual, or an ordinary person who is afraid of death (or life, for that matter) this book holds something for you. Common themes in *Quarks of Light* include the concept of unity, the power of light, the value of each life, and finding your purpose. From beginning to end, the entire set of events that led to Rob's heart transplant are miraculous. There are also lessons of never giving up, being persistent, and remaining hopeful, even in the darkest hour.

Rob had a massive heart attack, failed initial attempts at CPR, and fell into a coma. Apart from his miraculous, marvelous, and meaningful recovery, Rob was blessed with a powerful near-death experience (NDE) which revolutionized his way of thinking about self and others, including his neurologically impaired daughter. In the early 90s, while working on a thesis paper entitled: "A Biopsychosociospiritual (BPSS) approach to mind-body interactions," I became interested in near-death experiences. In that paper I described a variety of mind-body phenomena, including the near-death experience. I argued that an NDE simply could not be explained by a reductionistic biophysical paradigm. A much broader construct (i.e. BPSS) was needed to properly address this phenomenon (and others like it).

To understand this, consider this passage from the chapter "Into the Ethereal":

Knowledge of how the universe works is understood in a flash. I sense complex mathematical equations, along with their solutions, floating in the air, surrounding me. The nature of the universe and the laws that govern its design are elegant. To learn the answer to any question, all I had to do was observe.

Although I have never had an NDE, I can relate to what Rob describes. I had a similar experience in medical school, where I laid my head down prior to attending class and I fell into an unprompted trance-like state. In that incorporeal state, I had a sudden understanding of deep mysteries, was able to solve complex mathematical equations, and had a profound understanding of life in a way that had never been part of my conscious thought. Unfortunately, I was disturbed by my friend sitting next to me who interrupted with, "Wake up it's time for class." I could not remember the details of what I had just experienced, which was (and still is) frustrating. Fortunately, Rob's experience offers a more sustained glimpse into a dimension that transcends our senses and material paradigm. As Rob says, "The only language I could find was that the veil was lifted and I was given a glimpse into the spiritual realm."

This book is riveting from beginning to end. From life to death and back to life again (this time a more vibrant and enlightened one), and from an orb of light to universal light, Rob explains how transformational his experiences have been. This book offers deep insight and hope for those assailed by the vicissitudes of life. Faith is more powerful than fear. Light conquers darkness. Hope is a strong force, one that motivated a grieving wife, Melanie, to utter the words "Please save him. We have a special needs child, and she can't make it without him. They're very close and I can't do this alone!" Her desperate plea unlocked the doors of life, even though her husband had flat-lined and cardiac resuscitation failed. The on-call doctor heard this cry for help and pressed forward with fierce determination, and against all odds, until she obtained a slight pulse.

Rob didn't just survive, but he came out of that experience even more whole, and now has a special, multifaceted message for the rest of us. Looking back, faithful family and friends, a family pastor, dedicated doctors, helpful hospital staff, an encouraging employer, and even sympathetic strangers all became part of the fabric of Rob's life experiences.

Not only was he given a new lease on life, but also a new heart—symbolically, emotionally, spiritually, and on June 6th, 2016, physically. You are about to read intriguing experiences (not just physical) that come with possessing someone else's heart.

While there were many treasures that Rob brought back from his near-death experience, the most important was a true understanding of his daughter with special needs, Maria, and the pure love that lives within her. *Quarks of Light* serves up a deeper appreciation of life and how we are all connected.

Jean-Ronel Corbier, MD
Pediatric Neurologist
CEO and Founder of the Brain Restoration Clinic

PREFACE

I have kept journals throughout my adult life, and I have included excerpts which have been trimmed here for brevity, but neither embellished nor reworded.

Conversations have been constructed from journals and my memory. Everyone mentioned in this story had the opportunity to read the sections pertaining to them and make corrections if their memory differed from mine. Our dear friend, known here as "The Rev," has requested that we omit his full name.

The medical records documenting each phase of my journey are particularly extensive because I made medical history twice. I have consulted these records for accuracy. Thoughts that played out inside my own mind are indicated with italics. This story is recorded as I experienced it, and without embellishment. Some people may criticize it for being fantastical, while others may criticize it for not going far enough in one direction or the other as it pertains to religion. I can only share what I have come to understand—nothing more and nothing less.

1959 - 1966

THE GLOWING ORB

It has haunted me my entire life. Like hearing footsteps in the shadows, something always close behind, but never revealing itself. Was it an omen, a harbinger of good things or bad things to come? It seemed peaceful, so why did it stalk me from infancy to adulthood?

Was it somehow quietly controlling me? Animating my life without my awareness? It seemed as though I had the freedom to make my own choices and I certainly did, both good and bad. Yet in the belly of my being... it waited.

Where did it come from? Why was it there? Did every child have one, too? One "what?" I would not talk about it or tell anyone; they would think I was crazy. I never imagined I would have to die to find out.

I was the youngest of four boys, born to Italian immigrants in the late 1950s. Our circumstances were humbling. The booming steel town of Aliquippa, Pennsylvania provided my father a working-class job in the steel mill, which afforded us just enough for a small two-bedroom house, not far from the smokestacks that billowed out thick, black dust day and night, like unwanted snow that would descend on the neighborhood, leaving its mark on our porch and our clothes hanging on the clothesline.

My mother and I were very close. We talked about and shared everything... except what I saw that night in my crib. How could I share what I couldn't understand? At the time, my parents knew something odd had happened when they were awakened in the middle of the night by their toddler, giggling and aglow with wonder; but without another explanation, they dismissed it as a childhood dream, and on with life they went.

What happened remains crystal clear in my mind. I was about three years old and, since my brothers were much older than me, my crib was in my parents' room. My favorite sleeping position was lying on my back with my hands open, palms up at each side of my head. An open position, almost as if I was waiting to receive something—and receive it I did. Looking up into the darkness from my crib, a warm, brilliant white light seeped through the ceiling. It was an unfamiliar light form, not from a bulb, the sun, nor reflecting off the moon, but one all its own. It didn't shine on me, nor did it shine around the room, but, rather, it was contained in its own space, a small, formless orb of sorts. It hovered in the same spot, seemingly attached to the ceiling.

I laid there captivated, mesmerized, waiting for its next move. Like watching a bird pick seeds out of a nearby feeder, I dared not flinch and make it fly away. Then, effortlessly, it transformed into the shape of an open hand with its palm facing toward me. Seamlessly, it detached from the ceiling and began a slow, deliberate descent toward me. Almost as if it knew not to frighten me, it drifted down in the rhythmic cadence of an orchestra conductor's hand.

Then it stopped dancing halfway down and continued its descent like a parachute—slowly, deliberately, in a straight-line free fall with its target set: my right hand. It touched my hand, but unlike the sensation of a human touch, I just absorbed its energy and it became part of me.

There was no burst of light or physical change to my body, but something took place inside of me. I had a spontaneous reaction, gentle, warm, almost as though I brushed against electricity.

I jumped to my feet with ease, grabbed onto the railings of my crib, and began rattling them like a baby gorilla. It was the kind of whole-body laughter that only a child could experience, one without any preoccupation of the world or its complexities. It was as though I had no sense of self; it was a laugh of pure joy, unobstructed by the mind and radiating from my body. The light seemed to infuse my very being. It didn't come *from* me, but *through* me.

My parents began mumbling in Italian as they lay there in bed, but quickly fell back to sleep. I wondered why they were not jumping around and laughing too. Didn't they see the light? Why weren't my brothers running into the room to see what just happened?

After that event, my childhood memories seem blurry until the age of five. I don't remember much about life or its daily events, but I do remember my mother constantly telling me that I brought my father great joy. I have one glorious memory sometime around age four during Easter, when my father came home from the steel mill holding a package of yellow marshmallow Peeps behind his back to surprise me. I ran across our speckled linoleum floor at full speed to greet him, my feet landing on the throw rug in front of the kitchen sink, and my father carrying me into his arms as if they were a magic carpet.

Then a scene from my memory plays out like an old black-and-white spy movie where a secret agent emerges from the thick fog, revealing himself to a foe. In that memory, my oldest brother is carrying me to the neighbor's house. It's nighttime and I am in pajamas. What is the occasion? A sleepover? No. The look on my brother's face and that of my neighbor signaled that something was terribly wrong. I was being whisked away as others arrived. Little did I know, the Italian tradition of the time was to visit a dying man in his own home.

What funeral? I have no memory of it. What is death? Is it simply the physical absence of another person? These are concepts a child cannot begin to understand. What I did know was that something had changed. My father's death would be the turning point in my childhood.

Other than that Easter recollection, it's a straight line from the joyous memory of the glowing orb in my crib to the encroaching fog at age five.

After my father's death, I learned that I had been born deliberately to be his hope and his joy, to lift him out of pain and suffering. Less than two years before my birth, a dreadful day in the steel mill plunged our family into the ice-cold waters of an unthinkable new reality. My father was knocked off a platform by a crane, falling some thirty feet backwards onto a hot steel billet. It burned his back and crushed his kidneys. There was no dialysis or medical treatment available at that time for

4

damaged kidneys, so a slow poison began his body's tortur-
ous march toward death. Suffering, toxemia, and depression
ensued for years. Doctors even attempted electroshock therapy
to break the grip of depression, but nothing worked.

Finally, after all attempts at medical treatment failed, my
mother consulted our longtime family doctor to see what could
possibly help her husband.

"I've never known a man to love children like your husband
does," said Dr. Jones. "Have another child, Mary. It will give him
reason to live."

"But won't his condition affect the child's health?" my
mother asked.

"Absolutely not," Dr. Jones said.

And so, I was conceived.

It wasn't until age seven, two years after he passed away, that
I came to understand that with his death, I had lost my purpose.
Since my parents' intention was to create me for my father's joy,
I now felt an emptiness. It was not only the loss of my father, but
also a void of identity. I had been conditioned to react joyfully,
to entertain and conform. Now, without my father to respond,
I felt separated from the world.

There began my silent, relentless struggle, which would
continue all the way through adulthood. Who was I? Why was
I here? My search for self commenced. The only way I knew to
survive in a world that had become foreign, was to fall back on
the positive attributes of my personality that helped keep my
father alive. The die had been cast. This is who I was now. Or
was it? Something constantly gnawed at me. Even at seven years
old I knew something inside me wasn't right.

I even felt separated from my brothers, and to a lesser degree, my own mother. I was engaged with the family in daily life, but part of me was elsewhere. My connections to those around me now seemed peripheral. I had lost my identity. I felt like an outsider. Suddenly, the world became a scary and unwelcoming place. I no longer fit in.

But I had a secret: I was not alone. Whatever it was that infused itself into my being that night in the crib gave me solace, so I began to go within. This is where I lived my real life. I felt the orb's presence, but had no idea how to use it or relate to it. I knew it was always there, but how could "it" help a seven-year-old? I struggled with its meaning; how could a light turn into a hand and become part of me? What was "it" after all? The experience faded, but the feeling remained. That feeling of joy and peace was still inside me; but was it enough to sustain and shield me from a world where I no longer felt at home?

As fear and doubt set in, my body reacted accordingly. There would be no more sleeping on my back with my hands to each side of my head open to the world. Instead, I slept on my belly, with hands curled tightly under my chest, protected and withdrawn. I could never take the chance of that hand floating away—it was all I had left.

CODE BLUE

A few days after a minor surgery to remove bone spurs in my neck, I went to bed early to rest. For two years some unidentifiable pain had me cycling through an army of doctors. Through the process of elimination, they determined that bone spurs were the cause and outpatient surgery should make all the difference. At the age of fifty-six I was athletic, although chronically sleep deprived, and under enormous stress because of the care required for our beautiful daughter with special needs, Maria.

After drifting to sleep I retained only fuzzy glimpses of memory from the next hours, except for a series of distinct experiences that are so clear and sharp, I feel certain they will never dim with time.

Shortly after ten o'clock at night, my wife Melanie's sleep was shattered by horrifying screams of pain and groans in the darkness. Her first thoughts were of our daughter Maria, whose seizures would usually strike in the middle of the night, catapulting us out of bed and into an immediate fight-or-flight adrenaline rush. Half asleep, confusion and terror led Melanie down the hall to check on her, only to find Maria sleeping peacefully. As Melanie gained her senses, she realized the screams were coming from inside our bedroom. She had no idea what was happening, but my thrashing about in the bed drew her attention into focus. At first she thought it must be residual pain from the surgery.

This, however, did not seem normal. She called my niece, an emergency room physician's assistant, and held the phone near my face so she could hear my tormented groans.

"Aunt Melanie, something is wrong. Hang up and dial 911!"

The EMT driver arrived and did a quick EKG.

"It looks like he's having a massive heart attack," he told Melanie, "but we can't be sure until we get him to the hospital."

Fortunately, in the small town of Gastonia, North Carolina, CaroMont Regional Medical Center is only three miles from my home.

Once in the emergency room, lying on a hospital gurney, I was given a variety of medicines to stabilize my condition as they tried to figure out the cause. They transferred me into a room to be monitored, and, thinking the worst of it was over, my wife breathed a sigh of relief. She was sitting next to me when suddenly I sprang forward in what she would later describe as a scene reminiscent of *The Exorcist*. Sitting straight up in the bed, it was almost as if someone had grabbed my lifeless body by the shirt collar and pulled me forward with great force to get my attention. My eyes popped wide open and I screamed out the name, "Frosty!" before collapsing backward onto the gurney. The heart monitor flatlined and my wife tried to drown out its incessant beeping—the sound of death approaching.

"No, No, No! Don't go to Frosty!" she shouted at me in a panic. "Don't let him pull you to the other side. Stay here with me. It's you and me in this life. Don't go to Frosty!"

"Code blue" rang out over the hospital intercom, and in rushed Dr. Shiddhi Patel with a team of doctors who immediately began resuscitation procedures. I had gone into cardiac arrest. Melanie dropped to her knees and began praying out loud to God to save me, desperately, hysterically begging Him to intervene. Before she was escorted out of the room, she stood up and pleaded with Dr. Patel, "Please save him, we have a special needs child, she can't make it without him, they're very close and I can't do this alone!"

Medical records show that resuscitation procedures lasted for twenty minutes, including CPR, several defibrillator paddle shocks, and multiple doses of epinephrine, along with four amps of bicarbonate. I remained pulseless and unresponsive, the definition of "flatlined." The doctors continued working on me, but I was not coming back. My organs started shutting down and I was rapidly reaching the point of no return, when it's pointless to continue because irreparable damage to the brain is occurring.

Feeling deep sympathy for my wife, Dr. Shiddhi Patel pressed forward against the odds. Something inside Dr. Patel also seemed to be pushing her forward, and with fierce determination she continued CPR procedures, along with a vigorous sternal rub and intravenous epinephrine.

She obtained a slight pulse, but it was too late to save my heart. I had entered the realm of respiratory failure and cardiogenic shock. For any chance of saving the rest of me, they had no choice except to slide breathing tubes down my throat and into my lungs—I was on the ventilator.

The hospital chaplain came to Melanie's side to offer some comfort, but none could be found. Looking for spiritual direction, Melanie called our longtime friend and reverend who we affectionately call, "The Rev." He lived a little north of Pittsburgh, PA. It was three o'clock in the morning, and though he never answered his phone in the middle of the night, this time he did. After Melanie brought the Rev up to speed, she handed her cell phone to the chaplain, who emphasized that I had died for a moment and was now in a coma.

"Let me pray about this and I'll call back soon," the Rev replied.

Melanie had dark thoughts, but somehow she found the strength to start calling family and friends.

Sometime later, the Rev called back and said, "While praying, I fell into a dreamlike state. I was kneeling outside looking up at the sky and I saw what looked like a clear tube, a ladder of sorts beside me. I sensed God was at the top of the ladder, and realized how insignificant I was compared to Him. Then the Lord spoke into my spirit and we had a conversation. I pleaded with God saying, 'Bring him back, please bring him back.' God replied, 'Why?' I said, 'For Maria and Melanie,' but He didn't seem satisfied. Then I added, 'For Maria's caregiver, Autumn.' But still there was a void, a gap that needed to be filled. Then I said, 'Bring him back so he can fulfill his purpose.' At this, God seemed pleased." Before the Rev hung up, he told Melanie, "Rob is going to live."

The cardiologist on call that night, Dr. Ajay Bajwa, was en route when he was called for emergency cardiac catheterization. He found the blockage in my left anterior descending artery (also known as the LAD, or "widowmaker") and inserted two stents, but my heart had already sustained deep damage.

As the sun came up, Dr. John Carson was on his way to work, unaware of the challenge that lay ahead. He arrived to find his colleagues swarming around my lifeless body, frantically working to save me.

To increase my chances, Dr. Carson did a Swan-Ganz catheterization (a "heart swan") in my right pulmonary neck artery to measure my heart pressure. He also ran an intra-aortic balloon pump from my femoral artery in the groin and up into my heart to keep me alive. These were extraordinary measures, and not typical protocol for a patient in my clinical situation.

I would lay in a four-day coma, during which doctors and neurologists constantly monitored to check if I was brain dead. The first two days of the coma, medical records indicated "No progress. Situation tenuous."

Melanie called in neurologist Dr. Jean-Ronel Corbier for an assessment of my brain. Dr. Corbier, a nationally known expert in brain dysfunction, autism, and neurology, had been our daughter Maria's neurologist for the past ten years. His assessment indicated that I was not brain dead, but the extent of the damage was unknown. The only solace he could offer Melanie was, "It is in God's hands now."

The unknown became terrifying as my wife wondered, even if I did come out of a coma, what would be left of me?

My oldest brother, Lou, arrived at the hospital in Gastonia, NC, after driving through the night from Pittsburgh. He immediately recognized the dire situation at hand, and told Melanie he knew exactly what to do.

Although I was raised Catholic, I was far from participating in my faith or a church of any kind. But Lou didn't hesitate to call the only Catholic church in town and appeal to the local parish priest.

"I'm in a jam here," he said. "My brother is on his deathbed, and I need your help."

Shortly afterward, the priest arrived, anointed me with oil, and administered what is known in the Catholic faith as Extreme Unction. This last rite sacrament is only given once in a Catholic's life—when they are dying, to prepare the soul for its judgement before God.

On the fourth day, Dr. Carson anxiously paced the hall that led to the waiting room. What was the best way to tell an exhausted, bereft family that the time had come? He was straightforward.

"We simply can't wait any longer. If he doesn't breathe without the vent, well…" He looked away. "It's time."

This meant taking me off the ventilator in a do-or-die moment. Later he would describe it as "The most nervous I had ever been in my life."

As Dr. Carson began to remove the breathing tube from my lungs, I had the first awareness since going to sleep the night of my heart attack. I heard a voice.

"I can't take this tube all the way out until you breathe on your own!" the nurse said.

It felt like I was looking through a thick, foggy piece of glass into a room I didn't recognize. I couldn't make out any images, just verbal commands.

I'm choking on my own spit. I'm drowning. How can I breathe if I'm drowning? Why isn't she listening to me? OK, I'll say it louder... Suction me! I'm drowning here. I'm suffocating!

I screamed for help, but no one could hear me.

This is a nightmare! I need to wake up, but I can't. Why can't I wake up from this bad dream? I should be able to wake myself.

Then I realized that no words were coming out of my mouth; the thoughts were in my head. I was screaming for help, gasping for air as if someone had tied a plastic bag around my head, but no one could hear me.

Finally, I began breathing on my own and they removed the tube, but I had no idea where I was or what was happening. Still heavily sedated, I fell back to sleep.

The next day I woke to someone gently shaking me. A calm, baritone voice asked how I was feeling.

Lying flat on my back, I looked up. The first thing I saw became ingrained in my memory. It was an image that will forever make me smile and give me peace; a tall, slender man with a purple headdress wrapped around the top of his head and a bright, colorful tie nestled tightly around his neck. A full beard and mustache engulfed his face and perfectly framed his eyes. Even his beard seemed to have a purple hue to match his headdress. As he spoke with a warm smile, his eyes became almond shaped and piercing. It looked as though he held the hope of the entire world in his eyes. Language wasn't even necessary—his eyes communicated everything. They conveyed peace, understanding, and most importantly, love. *I must be watching a movie and this character is fantastic. Is he playing a guru in this film?*

The man spoke again and said, "I'm Dr. Bajwa. I put two stents in your heart while you were out."

A profound dread washed over me like an avalanche. Dr. Bajwa's face fell out of focus and seemed to drift backward as the sights, sounds, and smell of the hospital room overwhelmed my senses. His mouth was moving, but I could no longer hear his voice. Everything progressed in slow motion. The beeping sound of the heart monitor next to my bed slowed and reverberated like a gong inside my head. Nurses rushed around checking my vital signs. The room smelled stale and stagnant, laced with medicines and disinfectants that clogged my nostrils. The IV bag above my head looked like a gigantic fish tank, and I could feel its fluid coursing through my veins. My eyes darted across the room at the speed of light. It felt as if I had driven through a long, dark tunnel, exiting the other side into a new reality I no longer recognized. I tried to scratch my nose, but my arms were paralyzed. I couldn't move my hands.

I looked around the room and realized, *This is not a movie. I have awakened into a living nightmare.*

In one sense, I instantly knew the gravity of the situation. What would become of my life? How would I work? Who would take care of Maria? Was there enough money? How would Melanie do this alone? All the thoughts we deal with daily—the stresses that consume us most: money, job, security, the mortgage, and so on—rushed to my mind.

But as quickly as these thoughts came into focus, they left, and a new thought replaced them: "Frosty." Frosty was the nickname we called my brother-in-law, who tragically took his own life only seven weeks prior. I did not yet know that I had died or that I flatlined; I sat straight up on the gurney and shouted his name. I only knew that Frosty now consumed my consciousness.

I looked up from my bed as my wife entered the room.

Although physically weak, the first words I said to her sounded childlike and hurried, with a higher-than-normal pitch: "It was Frosty. He came to me, Melanie. You have to believe me. I don't understand it, but he came to me!"

Melanie's eyes welled up with tears as she reached over and caressed my forehead. "I believe you. I think you know after all these years together I would tell you if I didn't. It all makes sense now, Rob. You screamed out Frosty's name seconds before you flatlined. I knew the way you sprang forward with supernatural force and the way your eyes popped wide open, that he was standing right in front of you. That's why I was so hysterical. I was sure he was pulling you to the other side."

I began to cry thinking about how Melanie must have felt in that moment. A silence fell between us as we stared into each other's eyes, quietly contemplating what would become of us. Like always, Melanie quickly regained her strength.

"Tell me exactly, what did Frosty say to you?" she asked.

"He told me, 'I've made a big mess out of things and I need you to go back and help clean it up. Tell my family I'm in a good place.'"

Melanie was stunned.

"Only my brother would have chosen those words. He was always making a mess of things and never cleaned up after himself. My God, it was him!"

I remained in that childlike state. With the innocence and wonder of a newborn babe seeing the world for the first time, I told everyone what had happened.

"Hey, did I tell you about my brother-in-law, Frosty...?"

Not even the janitor escaped my tale.

That experience explained why I said his name instead of calling out the name of my wife or daughter. Frosty had taken his own life in the upstairs bedroom of his parents' house, where he'd been living at the time. The night he passed away, his mother asked me to go up into his room and look for a journal that might give us a clue as to what happened. I went up into his room seven times, sifting through a gruesome scene until I finally found the notebook that contained his thoughts.

Did he come to me in spirit because I was headed into that spiritual realm myself? Was it Frosty who pulled me off the gurney when I sat straight up? Did he want me to go with him, or just deliver a message to his grieving family?

Had my wife and a nurse not witnessed me coming up off that gurney shouting his name, no one would believe it; but it is noted in my medical records. Now fully conscious, I contemplated what happened and the chain of events that brought me here. My mind settled down and began to replay my encounter with Frosty. I was hanging on every detail.

I mulled over something else lingering in my mind, another aberration that took place during those twenty minutes when I fluctuated between life and death. I couldn't put my finger on it—it wasn't ready to come out. I had no choice but to leave it behind in the hope it would reveal itself later... whatever *it* is.

I refocused and tried making sense of my experience with Frosty. I struggled to articulate how the essence of a person is expressed in spirit. I didn't *see* Frosty, but rather felt and heard him. Much like a blind person who relies on their other senses, feelings, and emotions, capturing his essence was a sensory experience. As Frosty spoke I *felt* an incredible peace and emotional purity emanating from him. In life, he had a terrible anxiety disorder and eventually turned to drugs for relief. That, of course, led to more anxiety and turmoil as his life unraveled. But he was finally free. None of that anxiety followed him into the spirit realm. His words were childlike and pure, as if he lost all memory of his earthly struggles, torment, and demons. I did sense regret in his words, "I need you to go back and help clean things up." Frosty was not one to ask for help, which was a clue that the unknown street drug he took that night drove him to madness. In his right mind he never would have committed that fatal act. His last sentence was the most puzzling: "Tell my family I'm in a good place."

No other memories remained of my encounter with Frosty, but my mind was now fixed on his last three words. *A good place?*

Having been raised Catholic, I was taught that taking one's own life was a mortal sin, which meant you were condemned to Hell—no turning back. I can't imagine anyone describing Hell as "a good place." In fact, that "place" where Frosty was felt so good, I wanted to immediately return there with him after having awakened to *my* new reality. There was an indescribable peace and love emanating from Frosty and the realm he was in.

I had never bought into the religious doctrine of condemnation for a desperate, complex, and misunderstood act. Now I was firmly and forever convinced that this was a man-made assumption, not the statute of a loving God. This revelation gave me great and lasting pause. It felt like opening Pandora's box—what other erroneous assumptions had I made about the Creator?

Melanie and I always heard it is common for a deceased loved one to help you make the transition into spirit at your time of death. She remembered family members' stories, and I remembered witnessing my mother experiencing the same phenomenon days before she passed. As I sat next to her I watched as she stared peacefully into the upper left-hand corner of her bedroom wall. In the last year of her life, my mother lost her ability to speak, but in an eerie, hair-raising moment born out of silence, she gazed intently at a bare wall.

Then she said clearly, "It's my brother Ernest. He's so happy!"

I got goosebumps every time I thought about it. There was no doubt in my mind that her brother Ernie, who had passed away some months prior, was there with us. Nothing could break her gaze. She had the look of a child staring at a lit up Christmas tree—totally satisfied and content, but still anticipating Santa's arrival.

Not wanting to disturb the moment or Ernie's presence, I slowly approached the bedroom wall that drew her stare, and caressed it in round, circular motions. It had to be a portal, I thought, since I could see no image. "Is he inside here, Mom? Who else is with him?" But my questioning went nowhere. Those would be her last words before she passed a few weeks later. I could finally relate to my mother's experience. Never again would I suppress the power and mystery of the spirit realm.

The second morning after coming out of my coma, a beautiful, petite Indian woman with glistening brown eyes approached my bed. She extended her hand to greet me, but realizing I couldn't reach up, she placed her hand on my arm instead as she pulled up a chair. All I could think about was, *What petite looking hands this woman has...*

Instinctively, I clasped her hand and curled it snuggly as she introduced herself.

"I'm Dr. Patel," she said. "I was the doctor on call the night you came into the emergency room. I can't tell you how happy I am to see you alive."

Neither of us could hold back our emotions as she described how many times she almost lost me, and related some of the procedures used.

Suddenly the conversation got personal. She cleared her throat and said, "My father and I were very close, almost to the point of knowing each other's thoughts. I was pregnant with my first child, a boy, and my father couldn't wait to see his face. But six months before my son was born, my father died suddenly from a brain aneurysm. My heart's been broken. That connection to him seems lost. I've been bitter about that, my faith shaken, but seeing you alive gives me hope that maybe, just maybe, there's something more out there."

I squeezed her hand tight and realized her father's story was a catalyst, triggering the door of my subconscious to open... and out it came. Now I remembered it all.

While Dr. Patel and her team were trying to resuscitate me that night, a male spirit entered the room, repeating the same message over and over: *Keep working on him. Don't give up. You can save him.*

The puzzle unscrambled and I put the pieces together. I could hear her father communicating through me.

*Was this his way of letting her know that he was with her in spirit?
Did he come to help her? Is it possible he's always with her and she's
not alone?*

Although she may not have heard the words, I believe she
felt *something*, which is why she brought up her father. I believe
she picked up on the message; a spiritual prompting. Her tire-
lessness that night proved that something powerful was at work.
More powerful than sympathy or my wife's pleading. Something
deep inside compelled her not to give up, and the more she
spoke, the more certain I became. It's that same *feeling*, the
knowing that I experienced when Frosty came to me.

Is this the time to tell her my thoughts? I wondered. *Surely, she will
think I am crazy. After all, we just met.* I was unaware of how tight
I was clutching her hand, but I sensed it was making Dr. Patel
uncomfortable, as she gently withdrew. I was relieved. I needed
time to sort things out in my mind, so I decided to let it go for
now. As she pulled back, I noticed again how feminine and
petite her hands were. *How was she able to do CPR on me so thoroughly with those little hands? They look as if they would break apart.*

"I have to go," she told me as she rose from my bedside, "but
I'll come back again to check up on you."

In the days ahead, I came to realize that my life was on the
verge of ruin. Everything I had worked to build and protect was
about to collapse, yet all I could focus on were these mysterious
encounters with the spiritual realm. The experiences were so
profound that my mind shifted and reconsidered priorities.

At age fifty-six, I wondered, *Where have you been, Rob? What's
your life been all about? Why did you allow that silent voice to be
drowned out? The one in those quiet moments when your mind was
calm, constantly whispering that something in your life wasn't quite*

right. You never did find your real purpose, the one you were created for. Is that why you have never been at peace?

Beyond the pain of my daughter's endless suffering, something had been gnawing at my insides, a situation consuming me for my entire life, far deeper than any disappointment of what my daughter might have become if not for Rett Syndrome. This was personal pain and suffering, a secret history that only I could own, only I could resolve. I had rationalized that life's inevitable distractions got in the way, but now I wondered if I'd get a second chance to finally slay my demons and discover my true self?

While lying in my hospital bed, I recalled a vivid dream I had a few weeks before Frosty's death. I was in Mexico on business and my neck pain had become intolerable. The day before, as I walked off the airplane and approached customs immigration, several times I found myself leaning against the wall, sweating profusely in excruciating pain. A customs official approached me with suspicion. He asked if I was OK, then proceeded to pat me down, most likely thinking I was a drug dealer or had something to hide. I made it to my hotel room and fell asleep, when a terrifying dream soon came to life. I was on my deathbed and my brother Bill was sitting next to me. Bill is a well-known journalist whom I have always admired because he understands his purpose and lives life on his own terms. I was crying and telling Bill how I wasted my life because I never found or lived out my true purpose.

"On the other hand, Bill," I said, "you have lived and continue to live a passion-filled, purpose-driven life."

I woke up sobbing and totally drained. I picked up the phone and called Melanie.

"We've been through so much these past twenty years with Maria that I'm not afraid to die," I told her. "Instead, my greatest fear is that I'll die without ever finding or living my purpose. I feel like I was created to do so much more."

That dream has come true. There I was and now here I am, completely incapacitated with no hope for the future. The peace that Frosty brought me drained from my body, and in its place it seemed as though I was squirming under an iron blanket. I might as well be dead, I thought.

A raging torrent of thoughts and emotions streamed through my head so fast I was unable to process the feelings. Fear turned to anger toward God. This is a familiar pattern I have continuously repeated for the past twenty years, since Maria was born into a life stolen by Rett Syndrome. This multi-dysfunctional disease state is so horrible that only an evil mind could have conceived it. Now I was furious.

Why did you save me, only to continue my torment? What more do you want from me? What have I done to deserve this?

I finished thoroughly cursing God in my head and, while still immobilized, another unwelcome emotion attacked: self-pity. A few hours later, my brother Bill visited and approached my bed.

I looked up at him and said, "My arms are paralyzed. My heart destroyed. I can't work. Melanie can't take care of both me and Maria. Will you take me to a state where assisted suicide is legal and let me die with dignity?"

He crossed his arms, smiled, and shook his head. *No.*

SEEKING A NEW HEART

It was a cold February morning when I was discharged from the hospital. As the nurse pushed me toward the main entrance in my wheelchair, the automatic glass doors sprang open as a sign of freedom. The wind greeted me with a "welcome back to life" moment of crisp, clean winter air and the smell of fallen leaves.

The hospital transport van pulled up to take me to a rehabilitation center, where I would spend the next several weeks re-learning basic skills. The driver lowered the steel handicap ramp to ease my entrance.

"Now you just sit tight," he said with a warm, sympathetic smile. "After I wheel you into the van, I'm gonna strap the chair down to the floor so you don't move as we ride."

"You can put that ramp back up," I told him, firm and determined. "Just give me a moment. I'd rather walk down the steps."

Once seated, there was silence between us as I stared out the window, passing by the lifeless winter landscape, which mirrored how I felt on the inside. As we approached the rehab center, my driver broke the silence.

"Listen, man... I take people here every day and I can tell by the way you wouldn't let me wheel you up in this van that you're different. You keep that attitude up, brother, and you're gonna make it!"

The van door swung open, and I gave my new friend a high five as I wobbled down the steps, leaving the wheelchair behind.

I approached this day (and all the others) like a professional athlete training for the fight of his life. I remained positive and focused.

A nurse walked me down the hallway and I could barely make it 600 feet without gasping for air. Never in my life had I taken a prescription drug, but now they seemed endless; blood pressure meds, blood thinners, diuretics... they took a toll on my body and mind. I was constantly freezing from the blood thinners, dizzy from the blood pressure meds, and endlessly urinating from the diuretics.

Each new day for two weeks, I entered the large therapy room with other unfortunate souls whose lives had been derailed by a catastrophic health event. One woman, who suffered a stroke, caught my attention early on. She was at least ten years younger than me. Her husband and adolescent daughter were there, watching in agony as she tried to complete the simple task of grasping a spoon. I felt deeply empathetic for her—pain recognizes pain.

My mind wandered back to a day many years ago when Maria labored that hard to pick up her spoon. It would be the last day she could feed herself. I have been writing in my journal for years about the struggle of watching Maria suffer. I experienced bitter frustration and soul-crushing sadness as she tried to free herself, even for a second, from the maddening hand writhing associated with Rett Syndrome.

The room was filled with different devices and patients were assigned an appropriate routine, depending on our conditions. For me, it was a treadmill with a harness to prevent me from falling; a four-step, free-standing stairway to nowhere (up one side and down the other I go); finally, the most humiliating of all, a set of gym mats and a physical therapist who trained me how to fall and get up without hurting myself.

It struck me how I had been taking the simple things in life for granted, the gifts that were given me for free—this magnificent machine we call the human body and its ability to regulate itself without a second thought. Now I realized I had been guilty of neglecting my own health these past years, always focused on work and living in fear that I would never have enough money to keep Maria at home.

Health is the lynchpin that holds our lives together and gives us the ability to live a productive life.

Once damaged, all else crumbles. But I was determined not to allow that to happen to me. Now that I was conscious and in control, it was time to

HEALTH IS THE LYNCHPIN THAT HOLDS OUR LIVES TOGETHER AND GIVES US THE ABILITY TO LIVE A PRODUCTIVE LIFE.

bust out of here. Having read countless books on positive thinking and manifestation, and attended many high-priced seminars, I possessed the tools. My efforts were working. After my second week of rehabilitation, I had met my goals and was feeling my oats once again. I pulled out my day timer and prepared a list of priorities to tackle at work and home.

What happened next I did not see coming. Late one after-noon my ankles began swelling and my breathing became even more labored than usual. Not wanting to admit to myself that I was losing control, I tried to push it out of my mind. But by nightfall, fluid had gathered around my heart—I struggled to breathe.

I was overcome with fear and anxiety, and it felt like I was reliving the suffocating experience of coming out of my coma just weeks before. Instead of calling the nurse this time, I call the Rev.

"Rev, I can't breathe, something's gone wrong," I told him. "I'm dying. I know I'm dying."

"Calm down, Rob," the Rev replied, gently but sternly. "You're not dying. God did not save you to let you go now. There is a purpose in all this."

"A purpose?!" I replied, trying to catch my breath. "What purpose can there be in more suffering? I'm dying here, what the hell are you talking about?!"

"It's the Holy Spirit working inside you, demolishing your old self, drawing you closer to God. Remember when we talked about the Gospel of Luke? That we have to die so we may live?"

"I've already died, Rev, remember? How much deader can I get than dead?"

"But God brought you back to life, and now you're in the furnace of affliction so he can finish his work in you. This is a training period in your life, when God is using suffering and adversity to break you down and rebuild you. He is teaching you how to depend on him."

"Oh, how wonderful!" I replied with sarcasm. "Now we're talking about a furnace. You mean the kind you throw coal in to burn? Is that what he wants to do with me now, reduce me to a pile of ashes?"

"I know you're angry, but you know what I mean. The furnace is a metaphor for purification, much like burning the impurities or dross out of minerals to separate it from the gold."

"How much more purification do I need, Rev? When will this let up? You know I've tried to rely on God as much as possible these past years with Maria and it didn't work out so well. She's not healed, she's unchanged. It's been the strong will of Melanie and me that has taken her everywhere, done the work, cost us everything. That is the only reason she's still alive and now you want me to depend on 'Him?' I thought God was loving, not a God that demanded more suffering to get closer to him."

"Rob, listen to yourself. You're answering your own questions. All these years I've been trying to help you understand that you have never really let go of your own strong will, your ego. You've been relying on yourself while throwing in a prayer here and there. I'm not saying you did anything wrong trying to help Maria. Of course, we are called to care for one another. I'm saying God will not intervene unless you let Him in. He created you with free will, that's how much he loves you. Turn to him or turn away… it's always your choice."

"Well, I hope God's happy, Rev. I'm flat on my back again, I can't breathe, and I need to call the nurse."

Hastily, I hung up on the Rev and called the nurse, who immediately put me on oxygen and increased my diuretics. By morning my condition had slipped for the worse—I had congestive heart failure. Dr. Bajwa was consulted and he tweaked my medications, which helped me make it through the last few days of rehab.

Before I was released, they gave me an incentive spirometer, a device I blow in throughout the day to help rebuild my lung capacity. I also had to begin outpatient rehab in the hopes of recovering some heart function. This bolstered me, convincing me that I could still turn things around. That is, until a woman came into my room who I had not seen during my three-week stay. She introduced herself and pulled something out of a box.

"This is a defibrillator vest," she said. "It will shock you back to life should your heart stop beating. It needs to be worn around the clock, even when you're sleeping."

It looked like a bullet-proof vest, cumbersome and uncomfortable, the type a policeman would wear. I was silent and sullen as she strapped me in and handed me the instructions. I did not look at her, nor did I care to listen as she gave me information.

"Do you have any questions?" she asked.

"Yes. How will I know when this thing is working?"

"Oh, don't worry, it gives you two warnings. It will say 'WARNING, STAND BACK,' so no one around you is touching you when it goes off, because they would get shocked as well. So make sure you're sitting or lying down, because some people get knocked unconscious."

"You're kidding, right?"

"Well, no. Look at it this way... you have your own personal paramedic with you at all times—isn't that wonderful?"

This time, as I approached a set of automatic glass doors, their opening did not represent freedom. Instead, I was imprisoned by this straitjacket and its battery pack slung over my shoulder. With every step I took, the additional medications made me feel like I was trudging through waist-high, thick potato soup. The winter air was no longer crisp and clean, but rather heavy and wet. No matter how deeply I breathed, even pushing my chest forward like a Marine Corp sergeant, I couldn't get enough air.

I thought about what the Rev said just days before, "God wants you to depend on him."

This time, I had no choice, nowhere else to run. I was coming to the end of myself.

During the short ride back home, I sensed that something shifted inside me. There was no feeling of joyful anticipation of seeing Maria or of sleeping in my own bed again. I felt drained of the happiness that should have filled me at the idea of going home to Melanie and Maria. The three of us have been close, and Maria's light refuels my spirit every time I come home from traveling. Instead, I felt despondent.

February 24th, 2016, I decided to open a journal. During my time at the rehabilitation center, a girlfriend of Melanie's had come to visit and brought me a Christian-based journal, with a different aphorism at the bottom of each page. I had been journaling on and off over the years and it always gave me solace, but during this phase I'd been too focused on my exercise program to open it. When I finally did I was stunned by the first words I wrote, which

GOD IS WHAT GIVES US OUR IDENTITY. THE IDENTITY OF MAN IS THE ONLY REAL QUESTION ONE SHOULD PONDER. I WONDER HOW THE WORLD WILL CHANGE AROUND US IF WE EVER REALLY UNDERSTOOD THE POWER OF IDENTITY.

seemed to come through me, but not from me:

God is what gives us our identity. The identity of man is the only real question one should ponder. I wonder how the world will change around us if we ever really understood the power of identity.

At the bottom of the first page I read the printed aphorism:

Be strong and courageous! For the Lord your God is with you wherever you go.

–Joshua 1:9

Later that day, Pastor Eric from the Lutheran Church in Cherryville, NC stopped by to see me. Melanie's parents were Lutheran, and Pastor Eric conducted the funeral service for Frosty. He heard that Frosty came to me when I flatlined and was deeply curious about my experience.

We sat down on the living room couch. Sunlight poured in through the bay window. I adjusted my defibrillator vest and made sure the battery pack was charged. Pastor Eric seemed taken aback at the sight of me. We talked, and I expressed to him some of my fears.

"People of great faith are also people of doubt," he said. "Even Pastors tend to intellectualize the scriptures and think miracles only happened in the past. But seeing you today reminds me that we serve a living God of miracles."

After spending almost two hours together, he asked me if he could write a sermon about my experience, to deliver to his congregation the next Sunday. He invited us to attend and I agreed.

Melanie drove us to Cherryville that Sunday morning. Even though we had rarely attended the Lutheran church she grew up in, she told me that the entire congregation prayed for me during my four-day coma, and they were looking forward to seeing me alive. As we pulled into the parking lot, I asked Melanie to go in first. I did not want to let on that I was feeling dizzy and weak.

After a few moments, I gathered enough courage to open the car door, but my legs felt like rotted tree trunks, disconnected from their roots. I slid both hands under my right leg, just above the knee, picked up the leg, and with a thud, my foot hit the asphalt. I twisted my torso to the right and grabbed my left leg with another thud. Now what? I stared at the church's main entrance less than fifty feet away, but from my perspective it might as well have been miles. I sat there frozen, but I knew I must move. Finally, pushing myself up with both hands on the car seat in a rocking motion, I was on my feet.

Everyone had already entered the church, so I had to pick up the pace. Suddenly, less than twenty feet from the entrance I heard, "Warning! Stand back!" I spun around on my heels with my arms straight out in both directions trying to maintain my balance, frantically looking for who was screaming at me. When I heard the warning a second time, I realized it was my vest talking. I began ripping and pulling my shirt off, trying to disconnect the battery pack from the vest. After I disarmed the device, I quickly tucked my crumbled shirt back in my pants while walking into the church, then sat down in the pew next to Melanie.

From that moment, I no longer thought of the vest as my personal little buddy trying to save my life. Instead, it became a constant reminder of my frailty. It was now an adversary. My chest had remained sore for a long time since being paddled in the emergency room, and there was no way I was about to suffer through that again.

I'd rather die than live like this.

Melanie was always vigilant about keeping the battery packs charged, but what she did not know was that I would disconnect it before it could shock me each time.

Although it felt surreal hearing myself as the subject of Pastor Eric's sermon, he left me feeling inspired and I wrote this in my journal:

March 1, 2016

I'm not sure if it's me wanting to believe or if it's the Lord that keeps whispering to me, "I'm going to work a miracle in you, and you will give me all the glory—so they might believe." Come, Lord, may your will be done in my life. You love me that much that you brought me back to life, so I could fulfill my purpose before I leave this earth. I'm confident as I grow stronger, and you heal my heart and remake it anew, that you will begin to unfold my purpose in a crystal-clear manner that cannot be misunderstood.

On the sixth day of March, Dr. Ajay Bajwa referred me to a heart clinic in Charlotte, NC for further evaluation. The news was grim at best. Melanie and I sat stunned and breathless as the cardiologist reviewed my records and his forecast for my future.

"Let's get to the point and talk about the elephant in the room," he said, after a few disingenuous niceties. "Your heart can never recover with exercise, meds, or a cardiac diet. As a matter of fact, you need to stop exercising immediately. It's dangerous. Dr. Bajwa can no longer help you. You are quickly approaching the critical care stage, so I'm taking over your care, changing your meds and your regime. There can be only one captain on a ship, and that captain is me now."

"Wait, wait, so what are my options?"

"Well, a heart transplant is the only long-term solution. But hearts are in extremely short supply, so the immediate solution is an LVAD. It's your only chance for survival. Besides, a new heart can only be transplanted in a healthy body. The LVAD will help you recover while waiting for a heart, which could be years. I'm scheduling you in for an evaluation. You'll be spending several days here."

My throat tightened as I stared through the doctor. I somehow forced out one word—a question: "LVAD?"

"Left ventricular assist device. It's a mechanical pump that we insert inside your heart to keep your blood flowing. The wires from the pump will come out the left side of your body, just below the rib cage, and attach to a battery pack, much like the one you're wearing now. The device is very quiet and can be hidden under your clothes, and will keep you alive while you're on the transplant waiting list. But I must be honest with you, most patients don't get a heart."

Melanie and I sat bleary-eyed and silent, as his young, eager assistant led us out of the room to the registration desk. My evaluation was set for March 30th.

My condition rapidly deteriorated after that visit. I stopped exercising and only took short strolls through my neighborhood, constantly having to disconnect the defibrillator vest. It became even harder to breathe, especially at night because of the fluid buildup, so I slept propped up on pillows. The meds were increased to help remove fluids, and the side effect was a constant cough. This led to sleep deprivation and anxiety attacks. On March 15 I landed back in the CaroMont hospital emergency room for IV treatment to help remove the fluids.

In a cruel twist of fate, they put Melanie and me in the same room Maria had been in, too many times to count, while being treated for seizures. Painful memories surfaced of watching Maria being held down by the nurses as they frantically searched for a tiny vein to insert the phenobarbital IV to stop her grand mal seizures. The dimly lit room felt like a torture chamber, its negative energy was overwhelming. The walls seemed to be closing in, as if to crush us, mocking us, saying "Who do you think you are? You can't beat this." I looked at Melanie sitting in the chair next to my bed. Her eyes were vacant, like some evil wizard had her in a trance, her body wilting, being drawn to the floor. Something dark was trying to consume us. I knew we were both in trouble. Then, out of nowhere, these words came shouting out of me: "Stop!" Melanie was as startled as I was, and she sat straight up in her chair looking more like herself than she had in awhile. It felt like we had both snapped out of it. The ER doctor opened the door and hallway light poured in behind him, so only his silhouette was visible in the doorway.

"Everything OK in here?"

"Yes. Everything's fine," I replied. Later that evening I was released.

The next morning, I turned to my journal:

March 16, 2016

I feel so weak and thin-chested. Today is one of those days where I'm not sure it's worth fighting anymore. I cry out to you, God, please help me. I can do you no good in this condition. What will you have me do now? Why did you bring me back from death's door?

When will the horror of Maria's seizures end? When will my wife, who has endured so much, ever find peace? I'm trying to watch for your signs. As I sit here at my kitchen counter, light streams in through the window, its powerful beams infusing my body, giving me strength while I bask in its glow. But in a moment, it will be gone. Is this a sign? Are you showing me what we are made of? That flesh, blood, and bone have abandoned me? Is spirit the glue that holds a mortal being together?"

Every day leading up to my LVAD assessment date was marked by another physical setback. I began researching the complications associated with the LVAD and decided that for me personally, it was not an option. The second most promising treatment seemed to be stem cells. I gathered my medical records and sent them overnight to the country's foremost stem cell research center. Their response was prompt and decisive; my heart was too far gone.

The weaker I became, the more I emotionally distanced myself from Melanie, Maria, and her caregivers. I organized our files—financial documents, passwords, and insurance information. I prepared for my permanent departure, and left Melanie with clear instructions.

As I began getting my affairs in order, one afternoon a childhood memory stopped me in my tracks. Shortly after my father died, my mother was searching for a way to provide her family with income. With four boys to feed and no formal skills or education, she had to get creative. It dawned on her how much everyone loved her homemade bread, and the light bulb came on; she would bake bread and sell it to the Catholic church. A small business was born. But the work was grueling. With only one stove in our tiny kitchen and each batch of dough kneaded by hand, she was wearing down quickly. One morning while helping her with the baking, she looked more haggard and pensive than usual. Not understanding how desperate our situation had become, I asked her,

"Mum, why do you have to work so hard?"

She continued kneading the dough, not looking at me, knowing that if she did she would break down. The small wooden table covered in white flour creaked with each knead, providing a background rhythm to the story she told:

> "A long time ago in our family's village in Italy, there was a widow, much like me, with many children. They lived on a farm way, way out in the country. One day while picking her garden, she got bit by a poisonous snake. Knowing she was going to die, but not wanting to scare her children, she began canning vegetables, cooking food, sewing their clothes, and doing everything she could to prepare them. Guess what happened?"

I could see her face brighten up. I was relieved, thinking, *maybe there is a happy ending to this terrible story.*

> "The woman worked so hard," she said, "that all the poison came out of her body while she was sweating and doing her chores. You see, son, good things happen when you don't give up."

I put down the file folders and called Dr. Bajwa's office. I made an appointment to get a second opinion. Although I was no longer in his care, I longed for his comfort—he had always given me hope. My brother Lou, ever the father-figure in our family, insisted on coming, so he drove down from Pittsburgh.

We brought Dr. Bajwa up to speed and Lou asked him a pointed question: "Do you have children?"

"Yes," Dr. Bajwa said, "I have two sons."

"What would you do if this was your son?"

"I would take him to Duke University Hospital for a second opinion," he answered without hesitation. "I'll arrange the referral immediately."

That's all Lou needed to hear. He stood, thanked Dr. Bajwa for being so candid, and walked back into the waiting room. I stayed behind.

"Things are looking pretty grim, huh, Doc?" I said, my chin quivering as I held back the tears.

Dr. Bajwa raised his eyebrows slightly and his eyes seemed to twinkle, almost as if he was hiding a secret.

"Your future is not grim, Rob. You just can't see it yet."

I still had a sinking feeling about the LVAD, but it is state-of-the-art technology. I decided to move forward with the assessment, while waiting for my appointment at Duke on April 4.

Nothing could have prepared me for my three-day LVAD evaluation in Charlotte, which began March 30. The first procedure was a right heart catheterization. A hole is punched into the right side of my neck, allowing for a small hollow tube to be fished through the vein and into the pulmonary artery. The tube is left inside my heart to measure lung pressure and how much blood the heart can push through the body.

Outside the neck, the tube is shaped into a six-inch-high loop called a swan. That swan remains in my neck for two days, not allowing any movement, as if my neck is in a cast iron brace. It was impossible to rest. By the end of the second day, a surgeon from the heart failure team entered my room. I was sitting in my bed, propped up with pillows.

"Mr. Gentile," he declared, "your cardiac output is unsustainable. To keep you alive, we're going to insert a port, or PICC line into your chest. This line will drip a medicine called Milrinone onto your heart every few minutes. Think of it like STP, that fuel supplement to make your car run better. The downside is that it wears the heart out faster, so, to be clear, it's only a bridge until you get the LVAD."

It felt as if the room went black, as though I had been punched in the nose. My voice was muted.

"Do you have any questions?" he asked.

My eyes shot to the side. I didn't even want to see the name tag on his lab coat. Acknowledging his presence would make him real, and I was not ready to accept reality. Instead, I shook my head no, feeling the pain of the swan sticking out of my neck and hearing its tubing scrape against my pillow.

"Good," he said. "The PICC-line team will be in shortly to insert the port. In the meantime, I'd like you to just relax and watch some TV."

On the way out the door, he picked up the remote, turned on the TV, and there was a personalized greeting on the screen for me: "Hello Robert, we have some select videos just for you…"

How bizarre. It looks like they're going to sell me a timeshare condo in Florida.

Instead, it was a sleek, well-produced promotional film, showing various patients living their lives with the LVAD. It showed one woman, who was eventually able to return to her desk job, detailing how the equipment is quiet enough not to disturb her co-workers in the same cubicle. Then, there was a middle-aged man discussing how he became accustomed to the constant whirring sound of the pump forcing blood throughout his body at night. With the equipment staged on a nightstand in his bedroom, his wife explained how she was eventually able to sleep in the same bed again. The examples continued, ending with proper care of the wires extending out of the body and how to clean the perpetual wound and its constant risk of infection. I'm sure the film gave hope to many and bought them some time, but to me it felt spooky.

Now I was certain this option wasn't for me. I made my living traveling weekly as a salesman for a steel company. How would I possibly get on another airplane? And what of Maria? Melanie and I are up two and three times a night changing her diapers, dealing with seizures. I could envision myself hobbling down the hallway in the middle of the night leading to Maria's bedroom like Quasimodo, the whirring sound of the heart pump, battery packs hanging from my shoulders flashing red, all the equipment dangling and clanging—hell, it would be enough to scare *me* into having a seizure.

I made my decision—no LVAD.

It's better to lift this burden from my family now than put them through more suffering and financial strain. I'd rather stop the process than die a death by a thousand cuts. It's time to let go.

I was startled by a loud bang outside my door. The door cracked open and I saw a large, robotic mechanical arm with stainless steel pincers for a hand pierce through the opening. This soulless creature became more ominous as it revealed itself, squeezing through the doorway, slowly grinding its way toward me. Multiple steel arms with snaking wires, clear tubing, cameras, and appendages engulfed the room before it stopped at my bedside.

Then, in a birthday-party-surprise fashion, a perky young woman jumped out from behind this monster, a man in scrubs standing beside her.

"Hi, I'm Sara and this is my assistant, Eduardo." She motioned to the man. "We're the PICC-line team. This machine is like a live X-ray, and it's gonna help us find your veins so we can insert the port properly."

"Do what you have to do," I replied despondently.

The procedure begins, fails, begins, fails, begins, and fails again. My veins kept rolling to the side like earthworms that wince when you poke them. She tried multiple locations on my arm and chest. Each time I felt a searing pain that went all the way through me. The last two days of poking and prodding, the swan in my neck, lack of sleep, and the prospect of merely existing (not living) with the LVAD broke me down.

"Just let it go," I said. "I've had enough."

"What do you mean, let it go?" Sara replied incredulously.

"I mean, I don't want it. You can't get it in anyway, so it's not meant to be. I just want to be alone," I said, refusing to look at her.

Out of the corner of my eye, I could see Eduardo getting nervous, swinging his hands from front to back, while slightly rising on his toes.

"Eduardo, please give us the room for a few moments," Sara said.

"Sure," Eduardo responded cheerfully. "I need to get some extra gauze anyway."

Sara came to my bedside. The only light in the room was from the monitor screen hanging from the robot. She didn't ask my name. Instead she was direct.

"You got kids?"

"Just one," I told her. "She's special needs."

"Oh, that makes it even worse," she said, crossing her arms. "You remind me of my father, you know?"

"How so?" I replied.

"Shortly after I got married, my father started having heart problems. I begged him to go see a doctor, but he refused. I got pregnant with my first child right away, a boy. My father couldn't wait to take him fishing, and I relished the thought of watching them sit on the dock, chatting and laughing together. Instead, he had a heart attack and died right before my son was born. Turns out, one stent in his artery was all that was needed to save his life. I'm still angry at him, because he had a choice. Instead, he chose to leave us behind."

Lying there, my face bathed in green light from the monitor screen, her words "leave us behind" triggered a profound memory. When Maria was three years old, before the Rett Syndrome diagnosis, Melanie and I took her to The Institutes for the Achievement of Human Potential in Philadelphia, founded in 1955 by Glenn Doman. The Institutes is a nonprofit organization that created a program to help brain-injured and developmentally delayed people of all ages. One of its more well-known successes was helping John F. Kennedy's father, Joseph, recover from a debilitating stroke. For many like us, who could find no hope through traditional medicine, this was the last stop. On the first day of initiation into the program, the auditorium was filled with parents listening intently to each speaker while highlighting every word in our manuals.

The last speaker was Glenn Doman. Glenn walked across the stage, naturally commanding respect with every step, and sat in a chair. He was a gentle man, who looked exactly like the beloved Christmas song singer and actor Burl Ives, with his white hair, round glasses, and neatly trimmed white goatee. His speech was short, succinct, and indelible.

"In the second World War, I was a soldier. On the battlefield, we had a creed: If you leave the wounded behind, you leave your soul behind with them. All of you are here today because you chose not to leave your children behind. You have much to learn during your four days here. Godspeed."

His words never left me. They became *my* motto, tattooed on my mind, perpetually staring back at me, driving me forward.

Sara stood patiently, waiting for my response. My eyes made contact with hers for the first time.

"Go ahead," I told her, "finish your work."

Once the port was in, I never saw her again. By early nightfall, the Milrinone was dripping onto my heart as I laid in bed, shell-shocked and exhausted. I picked up the Bible Melanie left me the day before, randomly looking for an inspirational passage. An elderly black woman with unkept salt-and-pepper hair entered my room with a mop. Slowly, methodically, she swished it from side to side, her head down as if she had been beaten, never once looking up. I was thinking, *this woman looks much too old to be pushing a mop.* Surprising me, she broke the silence.

"Reading the Word, I see?"

I was caught off guard, and before I had a chance to respond she trundled over to my bedside. In an incredible act of intimacy from a stranger, she placed her wrinkled, calloused hand on mine and leaned in.

"You're a gift from God, you know. When you read the Word it brings light into this room."

I couldn't find words to respond. Instead, I raised her hand to my lips and kissed it. Nothing more was said. She simply walked backward, grabbed her mop, and faded into the hallway.

I returned home from Charlotte and opened my journal.

April 1, 2016

I spent three days at the heart clinic being evaluated. It was sheer torture. But what strikes me the most are the people in the trenches that I've met along the way. They are the real heroes. Or are they angels sent to encourage me? I'm beginning to wonder.

This aphorism at the bottom of the page made me do a double take:

My health may fail, and my spirit may grow weak, but God remains the strength of my heart; He is mine forever.

—Psalms 73:26

On the morning of April 3rd, I was anxiously awaiting a visit from the Rev. At my request he had driven through the night from Pittsburgh. I wanted to see him before my appointment at Duke, scheduled for the next day.

It was a beautiful morning, and we sat outside on the brick patio in my backyard, bathed in the early spring warmth. I noticed how the soft sunlight butters each brick on the patio, giving them texture and dimension. The ants were going about their business at my feet, and I marveled at these simple beauties that I'd never before recognized. My eyes were open to nature, but my body and spirit were flagging. Hanging from my right shoulder and flashing red every few seconds was the battery pack for the defibrillator vest. Hung on my left shoulder was the Milrinone pump, flashing green and making a whirring sound each time it dripped medicine on my heart. I was in a daze of sorts, waiting for the Rev to deliver some inspiring words or profound spiritual direction, when suddenly he burst into laughter.

"What's so damn funny, Rev?" I asked.

"Look at you. You look like a cyborg, wearing all this equipment, lights flashing everywhere, pumps going off. It's like you're out of a science fiction movie."

"Well, I'm glad you're enjoying this. You drove all the way from Pittsburgh to poke fun at me, huh? I don't get you sometimes, Rev. I really don't."

"Rob," he said empathetically, "I'm trying to show you that God has a sense of humor. He uses the circumstances in our lives to break down the ego, to draw us closer to him. Do you remember Psalm 23?"

"Some of it," I said. "I know it's a favorite of many, including my mom, when she was alive. Something like, 'although I walk through the valley of the shadow of death, I will fear no evil,' right?"

"Well, that's part of it," the Rev replied. "The part I want you to think about is, 'He makes me lie down in green pastures.'"

"And that applies to me how?"

"Because God knows you can't work and travel like this. He brought you back to life and now he's forcing you,

44

metaphorically, to lie down and take spiritual nourishment in his green pasture. That's what this verse is all about. Sheep are dumb animals; they would roam the desert and die if the shepherd didn't herd them into green pastures where they could eat grass and drink. Human beings are no different. We run around, living in fear, while all along God is using the challenges and circumstances in our lives to show us we don't control anything. He gave us free will. He won't interfere unless you let him in. That's how he works, always trying to free us, if we just trust and let go."

"Rev," I responded softly, like I was giving my confession, "deep inside me, I realize only God could have saved me that night. But my mind won't allow me to give up control. What am I supposed to do, lock myself in my bedroom and pray like some monk until God heals me? Look around, Rev, you've been coming down here for over fifteen years now, praying for us, blessing our home, anointing Maria with healing oils, giving us hope, keeping us from going over the edge. But what's changed? Maria's still sick, Melanie's burned out, we're constantly under physical, emotional, and financial strain. Now I'm at death's door, unable to help my family. What would you have me do?"

"You can start with being grateful that God saved your life. You've been given a second chance to grow closer to him in spirit before you leave this earth. In the end that's all that matters."

I thought about his words for a long time. Finally I responded.

"I don't know how you've been able to put up with me all these years, Rev. Thank you for not giving up on me."

The day passed too quickly, and the next morning the Rev got on his way home as Melanie and I headed to Duke University. My brother Bill drove in from Washington, DC to meet us.

I had a few quiet minutes in the waiting room at Duke before we met with the director of the Heart Transplant department. I turned to my journal.

April 4, 2016

Having breakfast with Bill, it struck me how wearing this defibrillator vest and PICC-line pump have helped demolish my ego. I can see now how the ego gets in the way of spiritual growth. Once the ego is pushed to the background, it makes room for the Holy Spirit to enter and direct you. There's a world of difference between the ego and confidence. Confidence, if you realize your identity as a child of God, comes naturally.

The director greeted us warmly, but he wasted no time, launching into a truthful synopsis about the world of organ donation and heart transplant.

"The truth is that hearts *are* in short supply," he said, explaining that hope begins to fade. "You must be in critical condition to get on what's referred to as the '1A transplant list.' Even then, there's no guarantee you'll get a heart. So, this is how the process works here at Duke—once we admit you, we'll fish a pump into your heart, through the groin, like they did that night in the emergency room to keep you alive. This pump is only a temporary bridge to transplant, in the hopes a donor heart will arrive. This is unlike the LVAD, which is permanent if you don't get transplanted. This temporary pump is attached to a machine about the size of a 55-gallon drum next to your bed. It means you'll be immobilized and in diapers for forty days. We'll send in physical therapists every day to work your upper body and change your diaper."

"What could possibly disqualify him from getting a heart?" Melanie asked.

"Several things," the director replied. "In the unlikely event that he has cancer, the federal government will not allow transplantation, because after transplant he'll be on immune suppressants the rest of his life to prevent rejection of the heart. Once the immune system is suppressed, cancer would flourish, since there's nothing to keep it in check. With hearts already in short supply, we could not take the chance of wasting one. AIDS would be another disqualifier, as would severe diabetes."

"Well, thank God we don't have to worry about any of that," Melanie replied.

I was unable to ask the next pressing question. All I could think about was how Maria must have felt at age twenty, depending on others to change her diaper. The thought of me having to defecate in a diaper for forty days was the final blow to whatever dignity I had left.

Bill said the words that I could not.

"What happens if a heart doesn't arrive after forty days?"

The doctor hesitated, then directed his answer toward Melanie.

"The LVAD would be the only option left."

I was sinking, and the walls seemed like they were closing in. It felt like all three of them were staring at me at once, waiting for my decision. It felt like a choice between death by lethal injection or electric chair.

Melanie read on my face that I'd already made my decision, and before I could speak, she broke the silence with a plea.

"Please give this a chance, Rob. We don't have a choice."

At that point I was a zombie, with nothing left to say. We were escorted to the registration desk to sign the documents and I noticed several LVAD patients waiting to see the doctor. I could feel their despair as they fidgeted with their equipment, staring blindly into space. My admission date was set for April 14.

The three of us made our way back to the parking lot in silence. As we approached Bill's car to see him off, he became even more pensive. There was nothing left to say. I gave him a hug.

"Safe travels, brother. Thanks again for coming."

Melanie drove us back to Gastonia and we said very little. We were both too busy replaying our own versions of the movie we just saw. I'm not sure what she experienced, but it felt to me like a horror film. That night I awoke from a very strange dream and grabbed my journal to scribble it down.

April 5, 2016

Had two other people on the back of a snowmobile, but could not make out their faces. We were trying to get out of somewhere. Mom was in the front with me. Saw we were caught in an avalanche. Mom said, 'Keep going, we can make it through.' I could only see snow and heavy mist in front of me, but we went through the avalanche and made it to the other side.

The next morning I called the Rev and asked him to interpret the dream. He had been studying dream interpretation from a scriptural perspective for many years. The Rev had always told me that God speaks to us through our dreams, through the prophets and our circumstances. He said he needed a few days but would get back to me.

On April 7th, I contacted my boss, Paul Chan, to update him on my status. Up until then, my employer thought I was recovering and would be returning to work.

"Paul," I said, cautiously, not knowing how he would respond, "I've been regressing. The best hope for me is a heart transplant, although that's looking impossible at this point. But the thing is..." Unsure how to say it, I paused, and words came tumbling out on their own. "Paul, if you put me on disability, I'll lose my insurance and could never afford a transplant if a heart comes available. I guess this is your Pontius Pilate moment."

"I will always choose life," Paul said, without hesitation. "Let me talk with the owner and get back to you."

The steel company I work for is a family business and Paul would speak with the owner, Michael Tang, and his two uncles, David and Audie. Paul called me back the next day.

"Rob, we've decided to keep you fully employed until you're well enough to return to work. We'll deal with whatever your capacity to work is once you return. Either way, we're in this with you for the long run."

"Paul, I don't know what to say..." I was so filled with gratitude I could hardly get words out. "How can I ever begin to thank you?"

Paul is not one to cater to emotions, and sensed I was breaking down.

"Let's put it this way," he said. "After twenty years with the company, you've earned it. Keep me informed on your progress."

Before I got a chance to respond, he hung up.

I didn't sleep well that night, and the following day I was so weak that all I could do was retreat to the guest room and try to rest. Paul's phone call gave me some hope that maybe God had not abandoned me after all. I picked up a little book a priest gave me—*Trustful Surrender to Divine Providence*—the same priest who read me my last rites in the hospital the night I died.

I thought about what the Rev had said on the patio: "*he makes me lie down in green pastures.*" It was the first time in twenty years that I was forced to stop dealing with Maria's care. As I pondered that, I remembered those ants marching around on the patio, and I realized that I was noticing things that I hadn't before. Why did those ants bathed in sunlight catch my attention? Now I was forced to be inactive with nothing to do but think and read about the power that comes from letting go. I felt in tune with my surroundings, as if something magical was unfolding. I put down the book and picked up my journal.

April 9, 2016

Sitting in the guest room reading 'Trustful Surrender to Divine Providence,' I have such peace. Listening to the wind howl outside and the power of nature. The perfection of spring pollination is awesome. The timing of the winds to spread seeds and to make the new leaves bud is proof of God's perfect timing. All this connects me to God like no other.

My cell phone rang, disrupting my writing. I saw that it was the Rev, so I decided to answer.

"Rob, here is my interpretation of your dream. I believe your mother is trying to tell you that somehow, you're going to make it through this. She's still with you and has a role to play. I'm just not sure where she'll show up next."

I thanked the Rev and tried to get back into that peaceful space, but my mind drew back to the night my mother died. She was living with my brother Lou while in hospice care. It was only a few days after Christmas, and hospice had given us the instructions to place one drop of morphine under her tongue in specific intervals, to ease her passing during the final hours. Lou, Bill, and I rotated duties throughout the night.

At 2:00 a.m. it was my turn to take over the morphine duty. My brothers began drifting to sleep. Bill had fallen asleep on the floor at the foot of her bed, while Lou dozed in a chair to her left, and I was on the right. Next to me was a small end table with the morphine bottle, an old-timey battery powered clock, a crucifix with her rosary draped over it, and a candle that animated the scene with each flicker. At 2:20 a.m. she began to breathe in shallow, choppy intervals. I placed the last drop of morphine under her tongue while clutching her hand, and at 2:25 a.m. it went cold. I woke my brothers to tell them... "She's taken her last breath."

I felt privileged to have administered that last drop of morphine. It was like old times baking bread in the kitchen, just me and her. Before my brother could turn on the light, I left the bedroom, not wanting to see her pale, ashen body. I wanted to remember our last moment together in the warm, soothing candlelight—one final, peaceful memory.

I picked up my book and attempted to get back to that place of just "being." But now I was distracted by the sounds of Maria and her caregiver, Autumn, in the living room. They were working on various physical therapy devices. Maria's own distinct form of communication is a combination of growling, chirping, and yelling, in no intelligible order. Feeling guilty about not spending time with Maria lately, I decided to leave the guest room to check on her. As I opened the door, I stopped dead in my tracks; something was not right. I didn't recognize this place. Much like an alcoholic becoming sober after a twenty-year fog, I realized for the first time that this house was in total disarray, with relationships damaged from neglect. I was awakening to my surroundings, and the scene was heart wrenching. I did a double take, looking back into the guest room; it felt safe in there, but I knew I must continue to step forward. I walked past Maria and Autumn, and neither seemed to acknowledge me. I wandered through the house as if I was invisible, wading around all the equipment scattered about in each room. Wheelchairs, large devices with harnesses to make Maria stand up to strengthen her legs for periods of time, heavy, clunky strollers with steel platforms to support her feet from the heavy weight of orthotics, a hospital bed with padded rails to keep her from falling out, a communication device that speaks various commands on her behalf in a dehumanizing robotic voice like: *Take-Me-To-Potty*. It felt as if I was walking through a house of horrors at the carnival, each room lined with mirrors reflecting the same abnormal, inescapable scene.

As I passed through each room it was more of the same. I walked past the den, browsing the pictures on the bookshelves. I realized that we have isolated ourselves from the outside world, held captive in here by Maria's seizures, unable to travel or participate in holidays with family or friends. Every time we did try to travel, we landed in the hospital, having to give Maria a phenobarbital IV to stop the seizures. Trauma and disappointment seemed to follow us everywhere.

Our wedding picture drew me in, and I examined Melanie's face.

Where have we been? It's as though we haven't stopped to look at each other the past twenty years. Always running, searching for a cure, trying to survive the daily routine. This is no life. We've been existing. You've tried so hard to make this a home, but it's nothing more than a rehabilitation center, and there is no end in sight. I'm so sorry for the way our life has turned out.

Maria's growling snapped me back into reality. I retreated to the guest room, the only room in the house absent of her devices. Despair washed over me; no book could pull me back or give me hope.

Even if you do eventually get transplanted you can't return to this, I thought to myself. *You won't have the strength to help with Maria. Who do you think you're kidding? Thank goodness you got that million-dollar life insurance policy when you were healthy. That'll be enough to get them through and provide care for Maria. Maybe you'll die before you get to Duke, and not have to put them through all this torment. Don't be a coward—you might as well submit to it.*

With only five days to go before my admission to Duke, I returned to the task of organizing my affairs and notifying my clients that I'd be on extended medical leave. While sitting at the kitchen table finishing up the insurance paperwork, on April 13th I got an unexpected call from Michael Tang, the owner of the company I work for. It was a watershed moment like no other in my life.

Michael's style was very direct—he had no time to waste, and got right to the point.

"Rob, I was at a board meeting today at the University of Chicago Medicine. I spoke directly to the president about your case and she's had a conversation with the medical director of the Heart and Vascular Center. Dr. Nir Uriel will be calling you later this afternoon. Just listen to what he has to say, OK?"

I was taken aback by Michael's personal interest in my situation, and stumbled on my words while both attempting to express gratitude and trying to wrap my head around what was happening in real time. I relished this fairy-tale moment, when out of nowhere some benevolent being grants you a last-minute stay of execution.

"Michael, I... I don't know how to thank you," I said, still in a daze.

"Just keep me informed," Michael hurriedly replied. "I have to run, but I'll talk with you later."

In disbelief, I called my brother Lou to share what just happened to me. I knew about the Tang Foundation that Michael's father, Cyrus, started, and some of the philanthropic efforts that Michael remained involved in, but all my years with the company I never really gave it a second thought. Moreover, I had no idea that Michael was on the board at the University of Chicago Medicine, nor was I aware that heart disease ran in the Tang family, sparing only Michael from the genetic predisposition.

Later that afternoon I got a call from Dr. Uriel. He has a thick accent and the background noise made it difficult to understand him, but his enthusiasm and positive energy were bursting through the phone crystal clear. He spoke to me respectfully, but with steely determination, making it impossible to refuse his offer.

"Mr. Gentile, I'm calling you from the cath lab—it's noisy in here. Anyway, I want to see you next week and start your transplant evaluation. My assistant will call you to get all your records transferred and schedule you in. If you don't have any other major health issues, I'll transplant you in three to four months. You will have to live near the hospital for one year after transplant, but we have a service that can help you find housing. You're not only going to live, but you will have an excellent quality of life again."

I couldn't believe what I was hearing. My first thoughts were of the obstacles, rather than the blessing.

How can you be away from Melanie and Maria that long? At least Duke would have been only a three-hour drive from home. What kind of housing can you afford in Chicago? What about a car, how will you get around? You can't maintain two households... this is crazy.

"The thing is, Dr. Uriel," I replied, "my insurance has been filed and they already approved Duke. I'm to be admitted tomorrow."

"Don't worry about that," Dr. Uriel responded without hesitation. "My assistant will handle the insurance approval for you. Cancel your appointment with Duke. I have to go, I have a patient here. But I'll see you next week."

I tried to respond before Dr. Uriel hung up the phone.

"But I can't just... wait, I'm not even sure if... let me talk to my wife and I'll call you right–"

I heard the dial tone and realized he already hung up. I lowered the phone from my ear, and stared at it. It felt as if I just got a call from Mars. I was stunned and mystified by the series of events, all in one afternoon, seeming to unfold at the speed of light. After coming to my senses, I called Melanie at work, expecting her to be crushed by the prospect of me living away for more than a year. Instead, she responded with joy.

"Oh my God, I can't believe this. Our prayers have been answered for once! I know what you're thinking, but don't worry about me and Maria. The caregivers will all pitch in. We'll find a way to make it work. Let's buy the plane tickets when I get home tonight!"

Before going to bed that night, I journaled the events of the day. The aphorism at the bottom of the page read:

Lord my God, I cried to You for help, and You restored my health.
Ps. 30:2

APRIL 2016

SELECTION PROCESS

O n the morning of April 19th Melanie and I were finishing
preparations for an afternoon flight to Chicago. Neither
of us had much to say. Our earlier gratitude was overshadowed
by the stark reality of my departure, not knowing if I'd ever
return, or if I'd see Maria again.

Maria was still asleep, and I was torn by the thought of having to face her. I'd been telling her for days what was coming.
Even though she can't communicate her thoughts and feelings
through speech, her eyes and spirit have always clearly spoken
to me.

While packing my suitcases—one for medications, pumps,
and batteries, and the other for clothes—it struck me how
painfully familiar this process had become. Taking Maria anywhere is an exhausting task—packing special foods, medicines,
orthotics, two pairs of shoes, mountains of diapers, wipes, and a
wheelchair. The tables were turned, and now *I'm* at everyone's
mercy. I'm the one with special needs.

Maria's caregiver, Autumn, arrived for work early that morning, and I greeted her at the door. I couldn't speak; I knew what was ahead of her as the lead caregiver. I clasped her face in my hands while staring at her, as if to say, *once you cross this threshold, there's no going back; I must know you're committed.*

She understood exactly what I was saying and replied like the tough street fighter I'd grown to love.

"Don't you dare start crying," she said. "I got this. Go to Chicago, get this done, and come home."

I was at peace with her response, and I moved aside so she could enter the house. At the same time, I heard Maria stirring. Typically, Autumn would get her out of bed, wash her up, and get her ready for breakfast. I shot Autumn a quick look that said, "Give us a minute."

I entered Maria's bedroom, shut the door behind me, and sat on her bed. She was lying on her back, smiling, staring up at me expectantly. I have seen that face before and captured it in a photograph more than ten years ago when she was still able to walk with little assistance. I've been carrying that photograph in my briefcase ever since.

The day I took that picture we had flown to Seattle, Washington to see world-renowned integrative medicine doctor, Dietrich Klinghardt. Knowing how much Maria loves water, we took a boat ride across the Puget sound between appointments. We let her roam around the ferry, enjoying the wind, the sun, and the boat's rocking. She was giddy, wide-eyed, and curious, exploring her surroundings with her back turned toward us the entire time as we followed behind.

Then, in an inexplicable, miraculous moment captured on film, she turned to look at us, and was made whole. It was reminiscent of a scene from her favorite movie, *The Little Mermaid.* With a touch from King Triton's three-pronged magical spear, she was freed from Ursula's den of darkness, spinning in a vortex, gathering light while being transformed back into the beautiful person she was created to be. Her eyes were filled with a sacred light that defied her body's brokenness. And that smile—it was the same smile I had come to know over the years. No matter how much pain she had been in, no matter how tortuous some of her treatment protocols had become, sooner or later that smile would appear, as if she was saying, "It's OK, you can't hurt the best part of me."

I curled up next to Maria in bed while caressing her face. I knew exactly what she was thinking. I thanked her for giving me permission to leave. Neither of us needed to say a word.

After Melanie and I made it through security at the airport, I couldn't wait to get on the plane. The onslaught of judgmental stares by everyone we walked by made me feel inadequate and less than human. To them I was some pale, ashen cyborg, with its lights flashing and pumps whirling—a burden on society. I wanted to scream out into the crowd *"Hey, don't you remember me? I'm a successful executive. I come here every week, I'm important—I have status, you know!?"*

But it was no use. I was becoming enslaved by the crowd's collective negative bombardment. It felt like their thoughts had become real stones being thrown from every direction, pummeling me into a pile of unresponsive flesh. I had to take cover, but where? Once at the gate, I sat down and began to focus on my shoelaces so intently that everything in my periphery faded away. It's a safe place, a trick I learned from Maria. I was remembering the day we came through the airport in her wheelchair and the TSA agent made me stand Maria up to examine her. We would always put two sets of diapers on Maria when we traveled, so she looked bulky from the waist down; enough to draw suspicion from the agent. As the agent stuck her gloved hand down Maria's pants, I could see Maria focusing on the spokes of her wheelchair, attempting to tolerate the indignation, while shrinking on the inside.

Now it felt like Maria and I were walking in unison, yoked together by our sufferings, sharing one another's plight.

After what seemed like hours, the boarding process began. I felt relieved to be in the safety of the plane, but it turned out to be more of the same. As fate would have it, our seats were in the back of the plane. The only way I could walk down the narrow aisle was sideways, with my arms spread out like chicken wings, holding pumps and battery packs tightly to my rib cage. With each row of seats that I passed, I glanced up in search of a pair of sympathetic eyes, while announcing, "Excuse me, I'm sorry, pardon me." Instead, the passengers curled inward in their seats, hands clasped tightly to their chests like they didn't want to risk any part of their body touching me. I might as well have had leprosy.

When Melanie and I got to our row, I took the window seat and immediately pulled out that picture of Maria. While staring at it, I became transfixed, motionless as the events of the day unleashed a cascade of painful memories. I was thinking, *How has Maria been able to survive the cruelty and indifference mankind has shown her all these years? I feel beaten down after a few hours of this treatment, let alone twenty years—what's her secret?*

Once in the air, I couldn't stop the flow of memories. My feelings were not my own; they somehow became entwined with Maria's. I was seeing things from her perspective. The flight attendant passed by and asked me if I would like something to drink as she tossed a bag of pretzels on my tray table, like throwing meat to a hungry lion, afraid to get close. This act of rejection caused me to think about the day we flew Maria to Seattle, just before that beautiful experience on the ferry. I had managed to get all of us in first class, so Maria would be more comfortable. After an hour or so in flight, Maria began to make her characteristic low guttural sounds, while aggressively wringing her hands. It's usually a sign that she's in stomach pain. While attempting to calm her by rubbing her belly, a woman seated in front of us, dressed in a leopard-print outfit, abruptly sprang out of her seat and began rummaging around for something in the overhead bin.

The flight attendant sensed that something was not right and immediately approached the woman.

"Can I help you find something?"

"Yes," she nervously responded. "I need my aromatherapy. I can't take it anymore."

"Take what?"

"That *thing* behind me," she exclaimed for everyone to hear. "*It* growls like a dog. I've paid for a first-class seat, and I'm not moving. Just put *it* somewhere else."

A man across the aisle leaned toward us and said, "I apologize for the way my mother-in-law is behaving."

His apology fell on deaf ears. The damage was done. Maria's growling intensified as she tried to drown out the insults, while focusing on the latch of her tray table.

The whirring sound of the pump dripping medicine on my heart snapped me out of this memory and brought me back to the present moment.

Why does society see Maria as having no value? I see her beauty and intelligence—it's just expressed in a unique way. Is this what we've become, judging one another's value as human beings by a set of standards created by, well… whom? Society as a whole? Who defines beauty? The media? What validates us? Our bank account, education, career? I'd give anything to know how Maria sees herself.

Once the plane touched down in Chicago, Melanie and I waited for all the passengers to exit before I attempted to move. I thought, *all I have to do now is make it to the hotel, wait for the sun to rise again, and I'll be at the University of Chicago Medicine.*

I was relieved this part of my journey was almost over. As we made our way through the O'Hare Airport, something peculiar was happening to me. It seemed like the terminal had become a sanitarium, filled with people who have special needs. My senses were heightened because of what I have experienced all day. No matter where I turned, a person with some type of affliction was standing in front of me. I felt like a pawn walking around on a live, interactive chess board, while some invisible force was throwing down a gauntlet of autistic faces, Down Syndrome, broken bodies in wheelchairs, all summoning my attention. *What is Maria trying to teach me?*

The next day, April 20, Melanie and I were in the waiting room of the Heart and Vascular Center at the University of Chicago Medicine. My brother Lou arrived that morning from Pittsburgh, minutes before Dr. Uriel's assistant called us into his office for our consultation. Few words were spoken between us as we waited for Dr. Uriel to enter the room. All of us had a glazed look of disbelief on our faces, as if we had been transported through time, wondering, *how did we end up here?*

I heard loud chatting in the hallway drawing closer. Before the door burst open, I felt positive energy approaching. Dr. Uriel entered, and he was exactly what I had envisioned after talking with him on the phone less than a week ago. Having dealt with hundreds of doctors, searching for Maria's cure over the past twenty years, I can easily sense the difference between a purpose-driven, intuitive healer, and someone who went to medical school with a different motive. He's focused on me only, temporarily ignoring Melanie and Lou for the first few moments.

"Rob," he declared, with arms wide open as if we were childhood friends seeing one another for the first time since grade school, "come, sit on this table and let me examine you."

As Dr. Uriel began to look me over and ask questions, the tension drained from my body for the first time in ages. I knew I was in the right place. Having reviewed my medical records before my arrival, he was more prepared than I could have imagined. He placed his hand on my shoulder.

"You got here just in time," he said. "After talking with you on the phone, even before seeing your history, I'm not sure how you have even been walking around." Dr. Uriel then turned to address Melanie and Lou. "I'm going to personally care for him. He is going to have an excellent quality of life, if nothing prevents me from transplanting him. However, I am concerned about family support, since he has no one here in Chicago. Transplant patients have the best chance of recovery with family support. He also has to deal with the emotional strain of having a child with special needs whom he won't be able to see. Because hearts are in such short supply, many factors are considered in the process of determining which patient gets a heart and support–"

Both Melanie and Lou interrupted Dr. Uriel, and began talking over each other, assuring him that ongoing support would be a given, with frequent family visits. Dr. Uriel seemed satisfied, and asked his assistant to admit me to my room.

As we said our goodbyes in the hallway, Lou surprised me with a revelation before his departure.

"I'm sure you don't realize it, but this is the same day our father died in 1964. You have always struggled with never feeling his presence in your life since he passed. There are no coincidences in life. This is his way of letting you know he's with you."

As I settled into my hospital room, the next few days were a welcome relief. The defibrillator vest came off and the pump was replaced by a portable IV drip. I was beginning to feel somewhat human again. Detached from these mechanical devices, I enjoyed the short reprieve before the rigorous transplant evaluation testing began on Monday. It was a Saturday morning and Melanie was distraught about having to return home. The only way she could reconcile leaving was realizing my peaceful state of mind.

"I don't know how you can be this calm," she said. "After everything we've been through, and now this. I feel so guilty about not being here every day to support you. Your brothers and I will come visit as much as we can, but for the most part, you must face this alone. Yet, you have that childlike serenity about you, like you did when you first came out of the coma. I don't understand."

"Melanie," I said with a smile, "I'm not alone. Your brother Frosty proved that to me the night I died, remember? Besides, Maria needs you now more than ever, and the reality is, we don't know how this will end, so keeping your job is really important."

Melanie teared up and nodded yes, reluctantly accepting my response as she finished gathering her belongings. After Melanie left, I grabbed my journal and wrote down what I really wanted to say to her in that moment:

April 23, 2016

It seems all human beings suffer from the problem of sustaining faith, sometimes from one moment to the next. Why do we lose our faith so easily when we struggle through challenging times and cannot seem to accept or recognize when God moves in our lives? We give control of our thoughts to the enemy of our soul when negative things happen, allowing fear and anxiety to darken our minds. The darkness dilutes our faith and blinds us to the power of God's presence. God showed up the night of my heart attack, working through doctors Patel, Bajwa, and Carson; it is so easy to forget after a brief period. Maybe what we think are faltering steps or weakness are really invitations to God's presence.

The aphorism that day read:

I know the plans I have for you," says the Lord. "They are plans for good and not for disaster, to give you a future and a hope."

–Jer. 29:11

The next morning I was more hopeful than ever. I realized my best chance for transplantation was to stay fit and not let my muscles atrophy any further. I developed a workout routine consisting of walking, standing wall push ups, and arm exercises with stretch bands. Blood draws each day began at 5:30 a.m., then I was transported for testing (sometimes in my bed) to various departments. Some days I didn't return to my room until early evening. After day five, my body began taking a punishment from the pace.

On Saturday April 30th I was writing in my journal when Dr. Uriel burst into the room in his characteristic, high-energy, style... but his demeanor was slightly off. I sensed that he was trying to hide his concern.

"Rob, you're doing great!" he assured me. "Everything is looking good, but your PSA test came back high. The prostate probably got irritated from the colonoscopy, but we must rule out cancer, so I've ordered a biopsy for this afternoon. We'll have the results early next week. I've got to run. Keep up the good work."

I was frozen in the moment, unable to respond as Dr. Uriel left the room in a flash. The words of faith I wrote moments ago in my journal were nowhere to be found. I placed my journal in the nightstand beside my bed.

"I'll be gone for a while," I said. "There's nothing left to say."

A nurse arrived and wheeled me into the urology department for a biopsy. The doctor asked me to lay on the table in the fetal position with my bottom exposed. I was prepped for the procedure by his two assistants, both attractive females, whose presence made me feel all the more embarrassed and humiliated. The stainless-steel tool entered my bottom, clipping small pieces of flesh from my prostate, while making a loud clicking sound. With each snip, the pain became more intense; but I wouldn't allow myself to feel it.

What is Maria's secret? Having watched her undergo thousands of procedures and trauma over the years, she continues to handle suffering with such grace. Does she somehow transcend her circumstances?

Tuesday May 3rd my brother Lou and his wife Carol came to visit with a surprise in hand. My niece, Teresa, a physician's assistant, sent a gift to cheer me up. Teresa and I had always been fans of Sylvester Stallone's *Rocky* movies, and even shared the soundtracks as workout inspiration. I couldn't believe my eyes as I opened the package. It was a reproduction of the exact colorful robe that Rocky wore into the ring in the first movie of the franchise.

I hung the robe on the curtain rail that separated my bed from the rest of the room, and gave her a call.

"Teresa, it's perfect. I can use the inspiration right now. It brings back so many good memories. Thank you."

"Uncle Rob," Teresa responded, with an unexpected stipulation. "You have to promise me that after you get your heart and you are able to walk, that you put that robe on and jog down the halls of the cardiac floor, doing the victory dance like Rocky did in that training scene when he made it up the steps with his hands in the air. Remember the song that was playing in that scene, 'Gonna Fly Now?'"

"Are you crazy, Teresa? No way I'm doing that!"

"Uncle Rob," she said in a serious tone. "You don't understand what that would mean to the docs and nurses who are caring for you. Those are the moments we work so hard for—that's why we're in this profession. Have somebody record it and send it to me, because I want to share it with the doctors I work with. Now promise me."

Because of my prostate I hesitated to promise her anything. But I forced myself.

"OK, Teresa. I'll do it."

As I hung up the phone, I heard several people gathering outside my door, but couldn't see through the privacy curtain or make out the voices. Something didn't feel right, like storm clouds were forming in the distance. I tried to ignore it, continuing to chat with Lou and Carol while keeping one ear to the doorway. My chest tightened and my palms sweat. I was hoping it was just my imagination, but the erratic sound of the heart monitor confirmed my suspicions.

I heard Dr. Uriel's voice and reluctantly rolled my eyes upward. Behind him were four sullen faces, their lips rolled in tightly as if sewn shut. I realized that in the past he stopped by with only an intern to chat with me, but today he arrived with the support of a silent entourage.

"Rob," Dr. Uriel began, his positive energy nowhere to be found. "The biopsy results came back, and you have prostate cancer. I can't transplant you with cancer, because when you get a heart you'll be on immunosuppressant drugs for the rest of your life to keep the heart from rejecting. Without a strong immune system, the cancer will flourish. To put it bluntly, with hearts in short supply, the government won't take the chance of wasting a heart. My hands are tied. It's a federal law."

I glanced over at Lou and Carol, all of us wide eyed from disbelief. I managed to whisper two words, as if I was saying them to myself... "now what?"

"I have to take you off the transplant list now and begin treating the cancer," Dr. Uriel told me. "The problem with that is, your heart is too weak for any cancer treatment. The LVAD is the only option left to keep you alive while going through this process. Once you recover from the LVAD surgery, we can treat the cancer or remove the prostate entirely. Either way, we'll have to wait another six to eight months after the prostate is treated to be sure you are cancer free, before I can put you back on the transplant list."

Once again, my head dropped halfway down, my body was drained of physical strength, and I was unable to speak.

"There is one potential option," Dr. Uriel continued, "but it's a longshot at best. If I can find even one person in the country who has been transplanted with prostate cancer and did well, I might be able to appeal your case. But we're dealing with the government. Even if we could get the approval, who knows how long it will take? Your heart gets weaker with each passing day, and we're running out of time."

I felt Dr. Uriel's genuine concern in his parting remarks, and I knew that he had grown to care about me, otherwise he would never go to all this trouble for a longshot. Then he signaled with a nod of his head toward the doorway that it was time for his entourage to leave. Before he walked out, he turned to me once again.

"This is not the path I had hoped for you, Rob... but you will live." He pointed to the Rocky outfit hanging on the privacy curtain and said, "Keep this guy in mind as we go through this process together. That's the kind of attitude I want you to have."

Not much was spoken between Lou, Carol, and myself as the doctors disappeared down the hallway. It felt as if there was a loud ringing in my ears blocking out all other sounds, like a bomb had just gone off in my room. My mind went back to the heart clinic in Charlotte. I recalled watching the sleek promotional videos of patients living with the LVAD and my intuitive decision that it wasn't right for me. Even though Dr. Uriel just told me the LVAD was the only way, I was certain that it wasn't the right decision. With this new diagnosis, I could be wearing it for years while I went through cancer treatment. I called Melanie to break the news.

"I don't want to leave you and Maria," I told her, "but I can't see a way forward. This path will take years. Years of long suffering and financial ruin, with no promise of a heart at the end. It's hard to believe we've come this far, but I—"

"What, what are you saying?" Melanie interrupted before I could finish my thought. She was calm at first, but became more hysterical with each broken sentence. "Are you telling me...? No, please don't leave us. Please don't die. I can't—I can't let you die. I'll help you with the LVAD. Oh, God, I'm begging you. You can't just walk out of there, they won't let you. What about Maria? I'm calling Dr. Uriel."

I sensed that Melanie was on the verge of a breakdown. She had maintained her strength through unimaginable challenges these past twenty years. Her weeping was so sorrowful, it made me realize that I was being selfish, taking the easy way out... ready to give up.

"I'll tell you what," I said empathetically. "Let's wait and see if Dr. Uriel can get approval before we make a decision, OK? I don't want to leave you and Maria, but I worry that my burden on top of everything else will be too heavy for you to carry."

Melanie proposed a dozen scenarios, ensuring that she could handle whatever the future held. Everything from an addition on the house, to my own caregiver.

Before we hung up, she told me softly, "I don't care what it takes... I just want to be with you. That's all that matters to me."

The depth of her love awakened something deep inside me. I was compelled to write Dr. Uriel an impassioned text message, highlighting the struggles we'd been through with Maria over the past twenty years, and how I would be an exceptional steward of my donor heart.

I ended my text like so:

"Please find a way to transplant me. I'll have the prostate removed after surgery, sign any document, do anything you ask of me, just please don't implant the LVAD. I don't have the means to live in Chicago for years, away from my wife and daughter while going through this process. Maria won't make it. I won't make it."

He responded, "It's an extremely complicated process. But I promise you I will do my best."

It was late in the afternoon when Lou and Carol departed for their hotel and I was more confused than ever, unable to get my mind under control. My thoughts were like wild horses running in every direction. I couldn't rein them in. I felt betrayed—betrayed by my broken body, and betrayed by what I thought was a loving God, who saved my life for a purpose. Realizing I needed to stop my racing mind, I focused on the ceiling, while lying in bed, and forced myself to sleep.

After a restless night, I pulled my journal out from the nightstand.

May 4, 2016

How, on top of everything else, could I have prostate cancer? This latest turn for the worse makes me wonder about the nature of prayer. Why are certain prayers heard, while others are ignored? I believe God heard Melanie's petitions the night I died and worked through doctors Patel, Bajwa, and Carson to save me... but now this. If Dr. Uriel does not find a way to transplant me, then what? Oh, God, let this pass over me if you are willing. Please give me the strength and courage to accept your will. I praise you and thank you. Please give me your peace.

No one showed up to draw my blood in the morning; no one carted me off to various departments. The pre-transplant testing phase had come to a halt, and now it felt like I was drifting on a raft with no land in sight. I was alone in my thoughts, bereft of God's counsel.

I called Melanie to see how her night was, because I knew she was on the brink.

"I'm so sorry," she sobbed. "You're going to find out anyway... I had a breakdown. I was at work when you told me about the cancer. On my way home, I called my girlfriends and my brother, Todd. They rushed over to the house and held me. I couldn't stop shaking. I was in trouble. I didn't want to burden you."

I realized the toll this was taking on Melanie. The conversation about her breakdown felt more like a confession, and it made me wonder how my brothers and their wives were feeling as they traveled back and forth to Chicago, lives interrupted, work missed, travel expenses incurred, emotional strain endured, etc. It was all piling up and I began to feel the weight. Maria's caregivers were also under pressure—especially Autumn.

Negative thoughts and emotions returned, this time mostly guilt. I realized the damage I'd done by continuing this fight. I took a walk on my floor with my constant companion, a stainless-steel IV pole with clear bags of medicine swaying next to my head with every step. As I passed each room I saw nothing but despair, so I decided to turn around. On the way back

I recognized a fellow standing at the nurse's station; he was wearing the LVAD. Since I was admitted I'd seen him come and go often. Out of curiosity I stopped and spoke with him.

"Hey man, you must like this place. What are you doing back here again?"

He turned to look at me, trying to muster a smile.

"They might as well give me a frequent flyer number," he said. "I'm always having problems with this damn thing."

After a long pause, I shook his hand.

"You'll never know how much you helped me today," I told him.

He gave me an odd look, as I trundled down the hall as fast as my IV pole would take me. When I entered my room, the Rocky outfit, still hanging on the privacy curtain, stared me in the face.

I folded it neatly and held it close. *"Sorry I let you down."* I tucked it away in the closet, shut the door, and painfully said goodbye to the contents inside. This triggered a dark memory.

In October 1999, Melanie and I had just returned home from The Institutes for the Achievement of Human Potential training. We both knew their program was our only hope to stem the tide of Maria's deterioration. It was physical and intense, and one of us had to stay home to lead the eight-hours-a-day, six-days-a-week program. After much deliberation, we decided that I would resign from my job and dedicate eighteen months of my life to the program.

I purchased three large boxes—two for my office and one for personal items. Methodically, I placed each item in the box while saying goodbye, allowing myself to feel and mourn every memory. I sealed the boxes with packing tape, and wrote "My

Life" on each box in black permanent marker, before sliding them into the closet. When I closed the closet door, I stared at it until my legs grew weak. To me, that closet had transformed into a coffin that I would not dare open again until Maria's program was complete.

Now, the sound of a voice transported me back to the hospital room.

"Hey sunshine!"

It was Geraldine, someone I felt connected to in spirit since my very first day in the hospital. She is a lovely five-foot-tall, positive ball of energy, with coal-black hair and eyes to match. She had become my confidante and I counted on her to explain why certain procedures had been done. When she thought I needed encouragement, she sometimes shared just enough within ethical boundaries to give me hope.

"Can you keep a secret, Geraldine?" I asked her as she sat by the window.

"Of course. You should know that by now."

"I have a plan," I told her, as I watched her smile vanish. "I've decided that under no circumstances will I allow them to put the LVAD in my body. As weak as I am, it shouldn't take long for me to die naturally."

"Do you have any idea what the transplant team is doing for you behind the scenes?" she asked me. She sat up in her chair. "Dr. Uriel is personally calling every transplant center in the country to see if anyone else has been transplanted with prostate cancer. The urologist wrote a letter encouraging the transplant team to transplant you first, then remove the prostate. The entire staff will likely vote to transplant if Uriel gets approval, so let's not talk about dying just yet."

"It's a longshot," I snapped back. "Even Uriel said that. Besides, no one can tell me how to die!"

"You're right. We can't make you do anything against your will." Geraldine gave me space to think. "I'll see you Sunday," she said.

"Maybe," I replied, as she walked out the door.

Over the next couple of days my mind was a muddy morass of negativity. I was so tired of riding the prayer roller coaster. Some of them are heard, others ignored. I was all prayed out. I was afraid that if I wrote in my journal, darkness would spill onto the pages, and I did not want to leave disparaging thoughts toward God that someone would read after my death. What would my family think of me?

This was not my first rough patch with God. Eighteen months after I packed away those "My Life" boxes I went back to work, and we moved to California on Maria's behalf. A team of doctors there thought they could heal Maria, but she only got worse. I developed a hatred for God, and turned to the metaphysical for a cure. When that failed, I fell into an all-consuming darkness. I documented those three years in various journals, both oral and written. Those journals had been untouched for seventeen years. I had been afraid to read them; afraid God would punish me for all the blasphemy. Maybe this was my punishment.

On Saturday morning, May 7th a weary-eyed Dr. Uriel walked into my room and shut the door behind him. For the first time he was alone. He gently placed his hand on my shoulder, just as he did the day we met.

"I got approval to transplant you," he said, matter of fact. "Not only that, but your case set a precedent, allowing patients in similar situations to be transplanted."

I tried to interrupt and thank him, but he continued, his voice more emotional with each sentence.

"Your case touched my heart, Rob. First it was the suffering you and your family have endured with your child and now this. You see, I'm a Jew from Poland. I grew up listening to my mother tell me how she watched half of her family murdered by the Nazis in what they called 'selection process.' The Germans would bring the Jews in by train and line them up outside. Then they would ask them, one by one, what position they held in society—doctor, accountant, housewife, etc. They would then determine on the spot, depending on what *value* they thought they had, who went to the work camps and who went to the gas chamber."

Dr. Uriel tried to hold his emotions and find the strength to continue.

"I promised myself that when I became a doctor, I would never practice medicine that way. Because everyone has value, and everyone has the right to live."

Neither of us uttered another word. He left my room, and I grabbed my journal to write while this was fresh. The aphorism at the bottom read:

Anything is possible if a person believes.

—Mark 9:23

I called Melanie and my family to break the news. Their reactions were so exuberant, supportive, and loving that it gave me inspiration to continue the fight. Maybe the curse had been broken. Maybe I'd been forgiven.

On Sunday morning, Geraldine bounced into my room, smiling so hard that all her teeth showed.

"Well, sunshine, I heard the news!"

"Yep, that's me. Call me Sunny," I said, sharing her joy.

"Now that you made it this far, your next step is to meet with Jeeves."

"Who's that?

"We all call him Jeeves because his name is so long. It's just easier. His name is Dr. Valluvan Jeevenandum. He's the heart surgeon who will eventually transplant you."

"I've heard about this guy," I said. "He's somewhat of a legend, right?"

"You can say that. He's personally transplanted over 1,000 people... including his own wife. You'll like him—he's very spiritual."

"What! Wait a minute, his own wife, are you kidding me? You'd have to be more than spiritual to cut your own wife's chest open!"

"He didn't want anyone else touching her, so the hospital granted him permission. You're right, he is a legend, and we're all proud to be part of his team."

THUMPER

The next morning, I was sitting in a chair near my bed reading and I sensed someone was staring at me. As I lifted my eyes from the page, I saw a tall, slender Indian man with salt and pepper hair standing before me. The way he floated into my room, I knew it had to be Dr. Jeevenandum. There was no need for a formal introduction, nor did he address me by my name. Instead, he pulled up a chair, dispensed with any small talk, and asked a question.

"So, what have you learned from your heart attack?"

I was taken aback by his gentle demeanor combined with such a deep question.

"What do you mean?" I was unsure where even to begin.

"I think you know what I mean... don't you?"

There was a long pause between us, then the answer came to me clearly, as if we had already telepathically communicated.

"Yes, I do," I responded. "I can't control anything."

"Exactly. Nor can I. Keep that in mind as we work toward trying to transplant you."

"Wait, *trying* to transplant? I thought I was back on the waiting list for a heart?"

"You are, but we don't know when one will arrive. Your heart is so weak, the goal now is trying to keep you alive until a donor heart becomes available, which is what I want to talk to you about."

"OK," I responded hesitantly, thinking he was going to pitch the LVAD.

"I've been working with a medical device company for many years developing a new heart pump. It's the size of a lunch box, so you can carry it around with you and remain mobile, not bed bound. It's called the NuPulse."

"How can I walk around with a pump fished up through my groin area? I mean, how does this thing work?"

"That's what makes this new technology so promising." Dr. Jeevenandum explained. "I'll implant a skinny balloon through an incision just below your neck, and I'll fish this balloon through the aortic valve in your heart. Attached to the bottom of the balloon is a wire that will come out of your left side, through a small tube just under the skin. That wire attaches to the pump box that you can carry with you."

"That's incredible, Doc. How many people have this pump in them?"

"Well, that's just it. Other than cows, there has only been one other person that's had the NuPulse, and that was done on an emergency basis. The patient only had it three days before his donor heart arrived, so we really don't know the long-term efficacy of the device. You would be our first human clinical trial."

My mind immediately went to Maria and how important clinical trials had been in the race to find a cure for Rett Syndrome. Each one has given new knowledge to the research, taking it one step further. This prompted the next question.

"Let me ask you, Doc... if this thing works, how many people could it help?"

Dr. Jeevenandum's demeanor is one of deep personal humility, yet he replied with quiet confidence.

"Not only will it work, but it will change the history of cardiac care. We envision patients going home with this device while waiting for a donor heart, instead of living in the hospital like you. And unlike the LVAD, we don't have to open the chest to install this device, so patients don't have to go through two major surgeries."

I was aware of the risk associated with clinical trials, but I felt an overwhelming sense of peace in the room.

"I'm in," I told him, without hesitation. "What do I have to do?"

"My assistant will bring you the documentation. Read through it carefully. Understand the risks. Once you sign it, we'll run you through a series of physical and cognitive testing before surgery."

After reading through the documents, I weighed whether to discuss the risks with Melanie. The two of us had always worked through big decisions together, but something told me I needed to sign the papers and not put this burden on her shoulders. Being a pharmacist familiar with clinical trials, she would almost be obligated to put her foot down. I waited until the ink was dry—my signatures firmly in place—before picking up the phone to call her. I explained the technology to the best of my understanding, and why I made the decision without her. Initially she was angered.

"I can't believe you did this without talking to me," she said. "I would never have agreed to it. There are too many risks."

I couldn't blame her, and I told her so. Then I did my best to convey that on a spiritual level I had a sense that this was the right choice for our family—I signed those papers to live, not because I was throwing in the towel.

There was a long silence on the other end. "...OK, I realize it's your best chance for survival. And I guess you're right, somebody must be first if medicine is to advance. But why does it seem like it's always us? We have been through so much with Maria, and now you... what is it with our family?"

"I've been trying to figure that out myself, Mel. I hope someday we have some answers."

There was an uncomfortable silence between us, both of us wondering how our lives came to this, both of us searching for strength, pondering what would happen if we didn't take the next step. I sensed we were each silently running those scenarios through our minds when Melanie broke the silence.

"Well, I guess I'd better take off work and buy a plane ticket," she said. "You're not going into surgery without me being there!"

Less than a week went by and Melanie arrived just before I was wheeled on my gurney into the surgical suite. She tried to disguise how nervous and tentative she was about the procedure, but her twitching and shaking told me otherwise.

The nurse stopped the gurney just short of the surgical suite and told Melanie she could go no further. Melanie leaned over to give me a parting kiss.

"The only thing I have left to hold onto now," she said, "is my belief that God saved your life that night for a reason. I'll be waiting for you in your room."

The double doors of the surgical suite opened slowly, and I felt the cool, purified air roll across me. My body tensed up. I could hear the squeaking wheels of the gurney rolling me in slow motion toward the center of the room. As I looked around, I realized this was no surgical suite, but rather a surgical theater. Above me, doctors were looking down, with their faces pressed into the glass observatory windows. Others were Skyped in on large television screens.

The gurney reached the center of the room. I was surrounded by gigantic surgical lights that looked like flying saucers. I searched for a pair of eyes that I might recognize behind the masks. I saw someone.

"Tim, is that you?"

Tim was one of the hospitalists I had grown fond of. His energy was calm and peaceful.

"Yep, it's me," he said. "How are you doing?"

"I'm fine," I told him, "but feeling a bit exposed. I didn't know the whole world was watching. Can you do me a favor?"

"Of course, what do you need?"

"Before you take my gown off and shave my chest, do you mind knocking me out first?"

"Oh, don't worry about that," he laughed. "Let's count to three together, ready, one, two…"

I heard a repetitive sound that I didn't recognize. It seemed to have woken me up. I opened my eyes and Melanie was sitting next to me.

"Melanie, what's that sound?"

Melanie was holding my hand and staring at me so lovingly.

"It's Thumper," she replied with a big smile.

"Who the hell is Thumper?"

"It's your heart pump, silly. You're out of surgery, Rob, back in your room."

I was beginning to come to my senses, but still in a dreamy state from the anesthetics. I turned my head to the left, and sitting on the table next to my bed was a small black box. There was a clear tube coming out of it that attached to a device implanted in my body, just below my rib cage. There was something natural about the rhythm: lub-Dub, lub-Dub, lub-Dub, yet also unnatural, as my body twitched with each corresponding sound.

Now totally awake, I realized it was NuPulse making that sound. I never thought about the human heartbeat before. There was something both magical and humbling about this surreal experience. Having a machine pump my heart for me, I realized how frail we are as human beings, dependent on this one marvelous organ to sustain life.

Coming to this realization, it's easy to understand why for centuries man has believed that the seat of the human soul resides in the heart. What if it does? If I ever got a donor heart, does part of the donor's soul come with it? My head finally cleared.

"Melanie, it's called the NuPulse."

"Not to me. To me its name is Thumper, because if I'm hearing that sound, I know you're alive. I have to say, you did the right thing."

The morning Melanie left, a nurse came by on her daily rounds and noticed that my body temperature was elevated. She advised the hospitalist to monitor my condition. By nightfall, I spiked a dangerously high fever. The doctor suspected I'd picked up a blood infection, and immediately began round-the-clock IV antibiotics.

Over the next four days I was stuck in a vicious cycle of high fever and chills. The intense dose of IV antibiotics induced severe nausea and vomiting. On day five I was struggling to breathe. An X-ray technician came into my room with a portable machine and confirmed my doctors' suspicions about my labored breathing; I had pneumonia.

My right lung was filling up with fluid and they had no choice but to pierce my right side and insert a drainage tube. The pain of impalement made it more difficult to breathe deeply. My breath was shallow and panting. That suffocating feeling overwhelmed me again. It was like I'd fallen into a murky fish tank filled with piranhas picking away at my flesh. I was trying to bat them away while swimming toward the surface, but I was running out of air.

Having only had a liquid diet for the past five days, my muscles were diminishing rapidly and I could see my body atrophy more and more with each passing day. The blood draws became more frequent for various testing, but no infection was found. Finally, the ultimate white blood cell nuclear imaging test was used to detect infection. Once again, no sign of infection in my body. My doctors remained confounded.

Late one afternoon, my brother Lou arrived for a visit and was shocked by how emaciated I'd become. Feeling helpless, he attempted to get my fever down the way our Mom did when we were children.

"I had no idea you were in this condition," he commented while placing ice packs around my head, "but it seems at the critical moments, our parents know when to send me."

The next day Lou returned to his home in Pittsburgh, and news of my deteriorating condition spread quickly throughout my family.

"I don't think he's going to make it," Lou confided to his wife Carol. "He has the body of a wizened old man and the voice of a child."

Alone again in my room, I picked up my journal.

May 22, 2016

I thought today would be my turning point, but the blood pressure meds gave me a severe crash. The only thing keeping me alive is my little buddy Thumper. I called the Rev and told him I can't go on another day like this. He told me to read and meditate on Psalm 91. As I look back on my life while reading that Psalm, I realize that everywhere I didn't put God first was a waste of time. I wasn't living as authentically as I could have, still justifying my own shortcomings, or what some would call sin. Is that the real meaning of sin? Not some ridiculous set of rules created by a religious institution, but not being authentic. This intense longsuffering, if you can endure it, peels you back like an onion, and what you find at the core is your true authentic self—where God resides. I also see, through it all, Maria has been the anchor that kept me at bay, never allowing me to drift too far away from myself, and drawing the best out of me.

By nightfall I was lying in bed, reflecting on my life while enjoying the view of downtown Chicago and Lake Michigan from my eighth story window. I had a corner room with a large bank of windows facing the city. A sense of peace came over me, but it felt forced because I was exhausted and too weak to fight. Once again I had no choice but to resign myself to circumstances beyond my control.

It had been a clear night, but as I looked outside, the weather quickly shifted. Dark storm clouds formed in the sky, crashing together in fierce howling winds and spewing sheets of rain that slammed against my wall of windows. That high up above the city, it seemed like I was in the center of the storm itself. Lightning bolts illuminated my dimly lit room.

Storm clouds rolled right up to my window and I was glued to the show; I'd never seen anything like it before. I watched the clouds transform into a shape. I blinked and the shape became sharper; it was a hideous human face. My blood froze in fear and I could not take my eyes off it. I knew that face, but I couldn't place it and I couldn't stop it. The more fear welled up inside me, the closer the face came to the window. I was too weak to get out of bed, but even if I had the strength, I'd be paralyzed in place. The face pushed itself through the glass window and, like a hologram, floated in front of me. Somewhere inside me a dam broke, and painful feelings of shame and unworthiness flooded in.

"Why are you coming to me now?" I called out. "Haven't I lamented to you enough all these years?"

Painful memories unfolded in my mind.

I was six years old at a department store, clothes shopping with my mother. As she looked through a carousel rack of shirts, I was at the pants carousel next to her, walking around and spinning it as I went. When I made a full circle, I came face-to-face with a boy about my size. We were standing so close I could smell his breath. His face was red, his skin twisted and patched together as if someone sewed pieces of flesh in the wrong places. His mouth was pushed to one side, a small hole with no lips. He had no eyebrows, droopy eyelids, and thin eye slits to see through. His ears looked like tiny conch seashells hanging just below his temples. It looked as if his face had been dunked into a pot of boiling oil.

I stood there shaking, unable to move. Blood drained from my head and I couldn't breathe. My eyes were open so wide I felt them burning. I didn't even realize I wet my pants until the boy's mother came around the carousel and looked down at me. She grabbed her son's hand and stared at me with squinted eyes.

"Come on, let's go home," she said as she yanked him away.

My mother, standing at the rack next to me, heard the commotion and turned her attention to the scene, just as the boy was being pulled away. She immediately realized what happened and shouted out in vain as they walked away, "I'm so sorry." They never looked back. She knelt down on one knee, put her hands on my shoulders, and gently shook me.

"Look at me," she said, "look at me! That boy has what's called a birth defect. No one knows why it happens, but sometimes it does. I've heard about that boy but have never seen him. Can you imagine how he must feel, how his mother feels? I know you didn't mean to, but do you understand what you've done?"

It wasn't until junior high school science class that I learned about Thalidomide and the horrible birth defects it caused. I have never forgiven myself for what happened that day; it's a pain I have hidden away.

The alarm bell on my heart monitor went off, and a nurse came bursting through the door, causing the boy's face to dissipate.

"What's going on?" she asked. "Your heart is in tachycardia. There's no reason your heart should be racing like this. I'm adding some magnesium to your IV."

The nurse finished her work, turned out the light, and closed the door. I was alone in the dark once again.

MAY 22, 2016

THE DARKNESS

Like a magnet I drew my greatest fears closer and closer. It felt like a malign force waiting to take advantage of my weakness. Was this just depression, or were the dark forces real? The little deformed boy from my childhood had come out of a forgotten dungeon and brought every rotted, shameful memory along to torment me. How did this memory escape? Who unlocked the door?

With the nurse now gone, I felt darkness return to the room and a conversation began to play inside me, almost like I was being baited by a specter.

"So, I see things have gotten worse since California. Your daughter is no better, and now you're going to die."

"Yes, I remember," I replied. "I have plenty of regrets. I'll carry those memories to my grave. I have prayed for forgiveness. But remember, I never fully gave in to you."

"Maybe you should have. Look around, dummy. See where prayer has gotten you? You're already in your grave! Let me remind you about *that morning on the beach in Los Angeles. You were so pathetic, bleeding knuckles and ready to vomit."*

"I remember all too well. I was desperate..."

The memory of that moment washed over me. It was so painful I have never before spoken of it. Maria was only four years old and had become a skeleton, unable to sleep, wild eyed, aggressive, constantly grinding her teeth, banging her head, and wringing her hands until they bled. We tried every treatment and took her to the best doctors, but they could do nothing for her. When traditional medicine failed, I embarked on an ill-fated quest for healing, trying unconventional methods as well. My frustration came to a head and led me to the beach that morning.

The tormentor jabbed at me again.

"Prayer never gave you an answer either. It only led you to the false prophets. Remember the "Saint" in Santa Monica?"

I do. People called this man a saint with the power to heal. We donated our money and he laid his hands on Maria's head while reciting some prayer. Then he put what he said was blessed holy oil on her forehead and said, "She'll be talking by morning." Maria woke early the next day before the sun came up. I went into her bedroom and tried to hold her, but she was uncontrollable, hyperventilating nonstop; it was maddening. She never spoke. While I held her, a rage I never felt before boiled up inside me. The move to California was our last hope; we had sold everything, risked it all. The medical community failed us, my home-based program failed us—religion, God, all of it. I never felt so deceived. Maria was cradled on my chest; it felt as if I was having a heart attack. I spewed venomous words, grabbed the picture of Jesus on her nightstand, and punched it until my knuckles split.

The voice kept after me.

"You're such a fool! Did you think a little canola oil on her forehead would heal her? It's suckers like you with your hard-earned money who keep those institutions alive."

"I was a fool," I responded.

"Now, get to the best part; the way we met."

The rest of the memory played out in my head.

I had put Maria in the bed with Melanie and ran down to the ocean a few blocks away. The beach was empty. I dropped to my knees at the edge of the shoreline. The water was ice cold; my chest was pounding; I could feel the veins popping out of my neck. I couldn't tell if the salty taste in my mouth was from my tears or the ocean water. I screamed up to the heavens with all my might.

"You've destroyed her! You suffered for a day, but you have crucified her for a lifetime! If you even exist, you will feel my pain when I spit in your face. Do you hear me?!"

I called out again and again, cursing in one breath, asking for help in another. I screamed until acid came from my stomach and burned my throat, while dry heaving and clutching the wet sand. I waited for a reply, but none arrived. That's when I called upon *any* force in the universe to help me.

The voice in my head jumped back into the conversation, gleefully narrating the next part back to me: *"You screamed out to the ocean, I'll use any force in the universe to heal her, just come to me now. I'm the one that heard you. I can help you again."*

"Yes, that's when you showed up," I replied to the voice.

I had not believed in dark power at first, because, like God, those forces remain hidden. But things began to change. My anger turned to hatred, which strengthened my willpower, allowing me to reject feelings of guilt. I felt a sense of freedom, free of this taskmaster, God, whom I had to worship with a set of rules from my religious upbringing. I believed that if I broke a rule, my prayer would not get answered. Now, free of those religious bonds, the more I relied on myself, the more confident I became.

I studied books on manifestation and spontaneous healing. I prayed over Maria, wrote powerful manifestation appeals, and meditated for months on end. I knew a breakthrough was on the horizon. All I had to do was focus my mind, connect to the infinite wisdom of the universe, and transfer that energy to Maria. If she didn't get healed, it was because my will and my mind must not be disciplined enough to tap and channel the energy into her.

I took her to "energy healers" of all kinds—vibrational, psychic, holistic, natural, you name it. One took a portrait photo of Maria and placed it into a machine. He told me he would make her whole through "distance healing" by transferring energy through electromagnetic frequencies, much like a cell phone uses. For the first time in my life, my mind was opened to other possibilities. My meditations became more intense, my mind grew stronger, and I was convinced that "I" could make her well.

I spoke to the voice again.

"There was only one problem."

"What's that?"

"She didn't get better."

Maria wasn't improving; instead she deteriorated before our eyes. Traditional medicine, alternative medicine, energy healers, manifestation prayers, nothing worked. Thinking she was autistic, the state even provided a team of applied behavior analysis (ABA) therapists, who came to our apartment daily and worked with her on communication. She never spoke a word.

My thoughts grew darker. Confusion set in. I was trapped. Having rejected God, I dared not pray. I had no choice but to remain in the dark. The world lost its color, so my memories of this period are in black and white. It was Christmas time; Melanie decorated a tree and commented how colorful the lights were this year, but all I could see was gray. My food was tasteless, and I lost my sense of smell.

A part of me was dying inside, shriveling up like the core of an apple left out in the sun. I wanted to feel alive again, so I drank more alcohol than usual; it numbed my pain and took away my desire to exercise. As my body weakened, my mind followed suit. I had strange, twisted, dark dreams at night, unable to meditate in the morning. With each passing day I became more impatient and irritated.

Melanie was frightened by the changes and challenged me. The more she challenged me, the angrier I became. Everything was falling apart and I was on the verge of bankruptcy—financially, spiritually, emotionally, and physically. Stumbling in the darkness, I forgot who I was.

"You misled me!" I called out.

"Don't blame me. I just use the laws."

"What laws?" I asked.

"Free will, you idiot! No good or evil force can make you do anything. It's always your choice. It's the perfect system. We both use it. All

I have to do is make the darkness more attractive. I plant the seeds of thought and let you do the rest. Your thoughts attract more of the same."

"Yes, it's a clever trap," I said. *"It starts out great, but one day you wake up and you're Gollum from Lord of the Rings. I had to learn the hard way that I couldn't manifest anything, that I couldn't create. You almost had me until I met one of your former students on the plane that day from Los Angeles to Seattle."*

"Which one?"

I was on my way to visit a client in Seattle and, once I boarded the plane, a man with a hardened, weathered face sat next to me. His wrinkles were so deeply ingrained they looked like a roadmap, revealing paths most of us would dare not travel. Something about his face reminded me of the novel *The Picture of Dorian Gray*. The more Dorian sank into a decadent life of wickedness, debauchery, and perverted sexuality, the more the disfiguring effects of evil showed up on the portrait.

I found it odd the man pulled out a Bible and began highlighting some verses—he didn't look like the type. I asked him what he did for a living. At first, his response was a little cryptic, but once he started there was no stopping him.

"I spent the first half of my life destroying people and the second half rebuilding them," he said. When I was younger I had the idea to start what is known now as assisted living facilities. They were nothing more than nursing homes, and I stuffed as many people as I could into a building. Back then there were no regulations. The conditions were bad, and I couldn't care less. My business grew, and I became wealthier by the day. The more money I made, the more I fell in love with myself.

"It didn't take long before I became addicted to drugs and alcohol—cocaine and vodka, my favorites. I bought a luxurious home on a large tract of land, and in the basement I had my own pornography studio. One night, something compelled me to take a walk through my backyard into the woods. It was there that I found the source of my wealth and power."

"What was it?" I asked, gripping the arm rest between our seats.

"It was my own darkness," he said. "Darker than anything I had ever seen. It was a pitch-black night, impossible to even see a shadow, yet I was emanating darkness. If light has a glow, then this was the opposite of that, and I came to think of it as *casting my own shadow*. I could see with my eyes how I could physically take the dark power I gathered and project it into the forest. Night after night I would go into the woods, just to see what my shadow looked like in the dark. I relished looking upon the power that I accumulated, showing up in the blackness of night. I had it all in the daytime, and after twilight, seeing this darkness gave me a feeling of freedom and power.

I stared at this man, and the hairs on the back of my neck stood up.

"Until one day," he continued, "on my yacht—that's the day the darkness was finished with me. I bought a yacht to celebrate my continued success, and one sunny day I sailed out into the ocean by myself to party. Once anchored in a private spot, I took off all my clothes to sunbathe, drank heavily, and snorted massive amounts of cocaine. I became dehydrated and passed out on the deck, flat on my back facing the sky. I laid there for hours unconscious, my body burning in the sun. When I awoke, I couldn't move. I knew I overdosed. I knew I was dying.

"To this day, I don't know where it came from, but something deep inside compelled me to scream out: *Jesus Christ save me!* At that moment I was given the strength to move. I rolled over, got up on my hands and knees, and crawled inside the cabin to radio for help. When I was released from the hospital I sold everything, went to seminary, and became a pastor to a small community church on the coast. What I know now is that light and dark are opposite forces, but the light won. The day the darkness abandoned me was the day I let God in. The dark force used me up and left me for dead. I didn't deserve it, but the minute I asked for help I was saved anyway."

The memory of that conversation never left me, and the image of that pastor casting his own darkness chills me to this day.

I spoke to the voice with renewed confidence.

"What do you have to say about prayer now?"

"That's a nice story, but prayer never worked for you. That's why you wanted to end her life."

"That's not true! You're taking things out of context."

The tormentor had me cornered and I had to defend myself, leaving me no choice but to recall the most painful memory of all. More than six months had passed since my encounter with the converted pastor. Although his story gave me pause, it wasn't enough to change my thinking. I remained disillusioned.

Maria's condition worsened. She had no quality of life, unable to sleep, passing whole food because she couldn't digest, and receiving the medical label "failure to thrive." The hyperventilating, teeth grinding, and growling were constant. She had devolved into a short-circuiting robot with wiring that was beyond repair. There was no way out. No matter what we tried, it failed. The burden was on me. I had to end the suffering for Maria… and Melanie.

I was too far gone to think about my own soul (nor did I care), but somehow, I had to preserve Maria's while setting Melanie free. The perfect plan came to me one evening when Melanie told me she was going to see a friend in Laguna Beach the next day. She needed to get away, and I encouraged her to go. My window of opportunity opened.

The next morning, before Melanie left, I told her I was taking Maria for a ride up the coast along Highway 1, my favorite drive, high on the mountain cliffs overlooking the ocean. Once Melanie left, there was no time to waste. I had to move quickly before I changed my mind. It was time for us to die.

I put Maria in the front seat of the car with me, intentionally leaving our seat belts unbuckled. We drove along the ocean highway, climbing higher and higher, careening around the sharp bends until I saw a section of road with no guard rails. Without hesitation I punched the gas pedal and over the cliff we went.

As the car smashed down onto the first edge of the cliffs, we were thrown forward onto a huge boulder, and the vehicle continued tumbling, breaking apart with each roll toward the ocean. Maria landed on her belly in what looked like a sleeping position a few feet in front of me. The boulder was tan and smooth. It seemed misplaced, as if it belonged in the desert.

Finally she was at peace, her soul intact and her innocence preserved. Her suffering was over... or was it? Something didn't seem right. She wasn't bleeding. I felt a sense of guilt and dread, unable to discern whether it was due to a failed plan to end Maria's suffering, or the fact that I just tried to kill my own child.

I crawled over to her, but I was unable to move. It felt like my back was broken.

"Oh, my God!" I cried out. "What have I done!?"

Then I noticed a flower that popped up through a crack in the boulder next to her head. The flower drew me in, and the longer I stared at it the more peaceful I became.

"How can this be?" I said. "How can this be?" I repeated that refrain as my focus shifted back and forth from the gruesome scene of Maria lying dead in front of me, to the flower. The flower offered a feeling of peace, which I focused on until it was all I could see. I felt as if I crawled inside it. Never had I seen a flower this exotic and beautiful. It had five huge petals and a stem that protruded from the center, with a tiny set of yellow flowers halfway up the stem, capping off with an even smaller bouquet of red flowers at the tip. The petals were deep purple with faded pink edges.

Wait a minute, I thought, *this is a tropical flower. It doesn't belong here. Something's not right… maybe we're both dead.*

Then I heard some loud, indistinct sounds that broke my concentration and pulled me back from inside the flower. As my focus withdrew from the flower, the scene abruptly changed. Flight announcements over the intercom system at the Los Angeles International Airport jarred me out of a horrifying dream. While waiting for a flight to a meeting in Pittsburgh, I slipped into a strange sleep.

I saw a man sitting across from me with a Hawaiian lei around his neck—there was my flower. I had been slumped down in my chair staring at that flower when I drifted into a trance-like nap, almost like a state of delirium triggered by extreme sleep deprivation and cumulative exhaustion. The man staring back at me wore a shirt with a clerical collar, and had a concerned look on his face. I wanted to say, *what the hell are you looking at?* But instead I asked (with a hint of sarcasm) "what do you guys do when God doesn't answer *your* prayers?"

Before he could respond, the boarding began and I was relieved. I was in no mood to be deceived by yet another phony making a career out of religion.

The specter was delighted by what I thought of this man in the airport.

"Finally wising up I see?"

"Let me finish," I said.

"Fine," the entity responded. *"Keep digging your own hole."*

There happened to be an empty seat beside me on the plane, and once in flight, the man with the lei around his neck walked up the aisle and introduced himself.

"Do you mind if I sit and chat?"

I reluctantly agreed. Turns out he was a Franciscan priest who belonged to a small church not far from where I grew up. His church was independent of the Catholic institution. He was on his way back home from a mission trip in Hawaii and the children had gifted him with a lei as a sign of gratitude.

We spoke mostly of Maria, her sufferings, and my disillusionment with God. But I remained guarded. I was not about to get duped again. We exchanged phone numbers, and to my surprise, he called me. A trust was forming between us.

That was the summer of 2000, and when we moved back to North Carolina in 2004, he would come to our home several times a year to teach us scripture. He became our pastor, and before long we nicknamed him, "The Rev."

"You're dumber than I thought. You let this guy into your home and after all those years of prayer and teaching, Maria's no better. Nothing changed."

"What changed through his teaching was me. I learned to recognize God's spirit."

The voice retaliated.

"You're still guilty. You planned her murder. Keep that in mind every time you look at her."

"I didn't plan it—I dreamed it. There's a difference."

I said the words, but still, my mind was consumed with doubt, shame, and unworthiness.

"It wasn't just any old dream, it was more like a fantasy. You had the thought, and you know that thoughts are the seeds of action. You might as well have done it."

My adversary's point hit home. That dream marked my lowest point. Is there anything worse (short of following through on it) than imagining a murder-suicide? This horrific dream is a memory that I have pushed into the recesses of my mind, too ashamed to share with another soul. Now reliving the memory, it felt as if I was falling into that tunnel again with no end in sight... deeper into the darkness. Despair began to overtake me when a new memory broke my freefall.

California was several years behind us, but Maria's condition was no better. Her digestive system was shutting down and her bowels were constantly getting impacted. To relieve her and stimulate her system to function, I had to give her coffee enemas, laying her in a tub of shallow warm water and hanging the enema bucket on the spigot, while kneeling over the tub.

It was a cold, rainy morning and I was feeling despondent and full of self-pity. The stench from her fecal matter that covered my hands was unbearable. My head hung low over the edge of the tub, down in the muck.

"God, where are you?" I called out.

Then I heard a voice clearly respond.

"Look at me, I'm right here."

I looked up at Maria. She had a glowing, peaceful smile on her face, and it felt like I was seeing her, really seeing her, with new eyes.

I snapped out of the memory and said these words aloud to my nemesis:

"For the first time in my adult life, I was certain that God existed."

There was no response. I was alone with my thoughts in my dark hospital room. The storm clouds outside my window broke up in the pre-dawn. A part of me wanted to remain in the dark. I wasn't worthy of the light. I felt exposed, as if my faults and shortcomings were tattooed all over me.

My strength was gone from lack of sleep and battling malign forces all night. I had just relived the most shameful moments of my entire life. Now it felt like everything had caught up to me—the relentless exhaustion of the last two decades, plus all the physical trauma to my body since my heart attack. I was drained, depleted, and spent. I let go and resigned my entire being.

With an agonizing groan I cried out:

"Do with me what you will..."

INTO THE ETHEREAL

In what felt like the next moment—although I cannot really say how much time passed—I was taken up into a timeless place. I found myself inside a shapeless, formless vacuum of sorts… an unending, infinite vastness. Much like looking out an airplane window on a cloudless day, I saw everything and nothing at the same time. I was everywhere at once, as if I was made of sand and someone picked me up and threw the grains of my being into a strong wind, scattering me across an infinite, timeless universe. I saw what looked like a hologram of my body in my green hospital gown suspended in space, while simultaneously seeing my broken, atrophied body in the same gown, lying in my bed connected to the heart pump machine that was keeping me alive.

What was happening is unexplainable. It felt as if I was connected to the vast wisdom of the universe—all of it, without words. I did not see a singular divine being; instead God was expressed as an imprint of concepts that I wholly understood without explanation.

I Am the power behind all things

My power is Omnipotent

I Am the origin of all

This is the Divine Source, the foundation for everything

This is your real identity

None of my body's pain followed me to this *place*. There was no machine sitting beside me pumping my heart to keep me alive, no tubes coming out the left side of my body attached to the pump. The IV's and needles were gone. This was just me and timeless space standing in the middle of nowhere.

The physical body's five senses had no functionality in this place where I now dwelled. There was nothing to smell, taste, or touch. What had been expanded was my ability to view light. The human eye can detect only a small percentage of the color spectrum. But in the Ethereal, unseen colors abound. Communication is telepathic. It is sensed, felt, then absorbed. It is extra-sensory perception and synchronicity at the same time.

I saw that time was only real in the physical realm to satisfy our one-dimensional linear thinking, but it was an illusion in the Ethereal. Instead, time was constantly in flux between past and present, creating the ultimate paradox. The future seemed hidden. If it was there, I had no sense of it, nor worry about it.

Knowledge of how the universe works was understood in a flash. I sensed complex mathematical equations, along with their solutions, floating in the air, surrounding me. The nature of the universe and the laws that govern its design are elegant. To learn the answer to any question, all I had to do was observe.

With each insight revealed, I thought, *Of course! How simple. It has to be designed this way. Everything is created from the same ingredients, same formula. All people, all creatures, everything animate*

*and inanimate are all connected. We just manifest physical forms dif-
ferently, but all things are one. This is the only way the Creator could
have designed it. Only humans have made it so complicated.*

I understood that I was not my body, my race, nor my
religion. This was a message of unity, oneness, and most importantly, relationship. This was my real identity. God experiences
and expresses himself through his creations.

Now I saw and simultaneously became part of what looked
like a gigantic web that covers the Earth and stretches to infinity. I cannot explain exactly what this web is, except that it
looked like it was made of trillions of neurons and it is a vast,
interactive network that binds us all. I somehow knew that each
neuron represents a life, and each life has a tiny quark of light
inside its nucleus. The dendrites or tentacles of each neuron
are entwined with the next one, weaving together a tapestry
of twinkling lights that hang on the ceiling of the universe.
Curiously, there were some parts of the web that are brighter
than others, while some were almost completely dark.

Suddenly I felt both exposed and free, realizing there was
no place to hide my actions (good or bad) in the universe.

I thought, *If I hurt myself, I hurt everything connected to me. But
if I love, the light will spread. I don't feel afraid or lonely here because
I'm connected to everything. How can I be alone when I'm part of everything? Loneliness is just an illusion.*

I realized I am part of a universal conversation taking place
in an unspoken language that all of creation can understand. I
feel this language is one of acceptance, unity, and love.

I became aware of myself hovering above my hospital bed
while looking down at my body. Now I began to observe the
nurses on my floor moving in and out of patients' rooms. It

was like watching multiple television screens at once, with each of their lives playing out before me like a movie trailer. It struck me that I was only seeing nurses that I had made negative assumptions about. I found it interesting that their lives were being shown in a regression of events. The film was going backward, from present day to childhood. It was like watching a cartoon artist draw each stage of a character's development on a separate page, then flipping through the pages at top speed to create the illusion of movement. Each time a life-changing event happened in that person's life, that page slowed for a millisecond, giving me just enough time to grasp what was going on at that time.

I was peering into their lives, observing their mistakes and watershed events, both good and bad, that brought them to this place. Anytime something destructive happened, like abuse, bad personal choices, or circumstances beyond their control, it has contributed to this moment, revealing a portrait of who this person has become.

Now, overwhelming feelings of their collective pain and sufferings became part of me. The weight of this seemed to darken my spirit, and I felt the impact. At the same time, as though on a different screen, my own life was presented to me. Here I saw mistakes about which I felt the most shame.

I thought, *How could I have judged others so harshly? How could I have judged myself so harshly for my own shortcomings?*

Then I saw Maria.

She was perfect and whole, staring at me with eyes filled with light. This is not the kind of light we see in the natural world, but a spirit of light that animates all life. She had a knowing smile on her face, the same smile I had seen so many times in our darkest moments together. I immediately recognized *that* smile. This moment confirmed what I sensed in the physical realm.

When I saw that smile again here, I knew the truth at once. The smile was a clue to the fact that she had always been perfect in the spiritual realm. Even through all the dark times she never suffered in spirit.

Now I communicated with her in the unspoken language of the Ethereal: *Please speak to me, I have never heard your voice. How I long to know your thoughts and your personality, to hear you say just once, "I love you, Daddy." Maria, I don't know what to do when you're having seizures. How do I comfort you? We have tried everything to heal you... what more can we do?*

Maria replied in a silent voice: *Just love me.*

For the first time in my life, I felt free, forgiven, and unburdened.

I spoke into the vastness and heard my own voice echo back to me.

I never want to leave this place.

The next moment, the whirling sound of Thumper pumping my heart came into focus. Now I had an awareness of the tubes and wires coming out of my body. I was back in my hospital bed.

It didn't seem to matter whether or not I received a donor heart. I now knew what awaits me even more than when I met Frosty. I wanted to get back to that place, to see my daughter whole again, and to be one with everything. I wanted to be in the eternal presence of God. As I lay there stuck in my broken body, my mind raced out of control, trying to process what just happened. The only language I could find was that the veil was lifted and I was given a glimpse into the spiritual realm.

How can I begin to explain this supernatural encounter? I sensed that some details were already slipping away from me. How could I understand everything in one moment, while in that place, through some sort of spiritual osmosis? How could I understand the Creator's design, but not retain the details?

My mind turned to a question: *Why have I been brought back to life? Why did Frosty come to me the night I died while the other male spirit cheered on Dr. Patel to save me? What is behind these mysterious circumstances which brought me to Chicago to get a heart? What was the purpose of seeing Maria whole in spirit while remaining broken in the physical realm?*

I heard an answer from God that clearly and unmistakably spoke to my entire being. It felt the same as that morning long ago when I was cleansing Maria in the tub. Just one word: *Testify.*

My faith was restored. No doctor had to tell me that a perfect heart was going to arrive on time. I would live to testify and to tell my story. All I had to do was trust. Trust that God had a plan and that, out of love, God worked all things for good. Trust that I would be given the words to explain the unexplainable when the time was right.

Melanie arrived on May 30th, and she stepped in to explain something about my medical history of hyper inflammation, which she believed was causing the problem, not an infection. Her medical background as a pharmacist was a tremendous asset in her ability to communicate well in these situations. When she consulted with Dr. Uriel, he concurred and immediately decided to begin IV steroids. Within two days my fever cycle broke, my immune markers declined, and blood work showed no sign of infection. My body was ready to receive a heart.

Melanie had to return home to work, and I could tell she was concerned by the shift in my attitude. I couldn't find the words to explain what I had experienced, but that childlike peace came over me again—that same peace I had coming out of my coma when I first met Frosty.

Melanie asked me several questions at once: "Why aren't you upset? What are you thinking? Are you giving up?"

The only response I could give was, "It's All Good..."

I later learned that Melaine told her best friend, Susan, that, given my physical condition, she was preparing for me to die.

On Wednesday June 1st, while waiting for my brother Bill to arrive for a visit, I pulled out my journal and began writing.

Dr. Uriel entered my room. Once again, he was alone, and he got straight to the point.

"Rob, you're getting weaker, and I'm concerned. I want to give you this option. There's a heart coming available tomorrow, but it's considerably smaller. You might get four to five years out of it, or you can take the chance of continuing to wait."

Dr. Uriel and I had been on a first name basis for a while now and I contemplated sharing the experience I had. Somehow, though, I couldn't find the words to explain it. I had not even been able to express this "knowing" that I had to Melanie when she was here, nor could I find the words to discuss it with Bill.

Instead, I responded the best I could.

"Nir, something doesn't feel right about that heart. Besides, I've been through too much to settle for less now—I'll wait."

Nir simply nodded his head yes, and with a half-smile said, "OK."

As he walked out of the room, I glanced down at my open journal.

The aphorism read:

Do not be afraid or discouraged, for the Lord will personally go ahead of you.

–Deut. 31:8

In the early afternoon on Sunday June 5th, Jason, one of my favorite physician's assistants, walked into my room. Cell phone in hand, he extended his arm toward me.

"It's my boss, Dr. Uriel... he wants to talk with you."

I stared at Jason, hesitating for a moment to take the phone from his hand. *Maybe they changed their mind about transplanting me because of my cancer.*

Before Dr. Uriel began talking, I could feel his positive energy bursting through the phone, much like I felt it coming down the hallway the first day we met.

"Rob!" he declared, "This is the moment we've been waiting for. Your heart has arrived and it's the perfect heart for you. You'll go into surgery at approximately 2:30 a.m. I'll see you sometime after the transplant in the ICU."

The phone felt glued to my ear. I couldn't move it or respond. I was standing in front of my window, staring out at downtown Chicago, and feeling the sun on my face. The "knowing" that I was going to live, which I experienced in the spiritual realm, had just been confirmed. I felt a sense of joy and peace that cannot be described.

"Nir, I will never be able to thank you enough for what you have done for me..."

That's all I could say. I handed the phone back to Jason, and walked over to my brother, Bill. I laid my head in his chest. Heaving a deep sigh of relief, my tears refused to fall.

"Congratulations, brother, you made it!" he said, with a warm embrace. "You better call Melanie to see if she can get a flight up here."

Melanie caught the last flight out of Charlotte and arrived at 11:30 p.m. Bill left the room to give us privacy, and she gently crawled into my hospital bed. We held each other until they came to take me to surgery. Melanie was shaking and crying the entire time—I smiled. I was at peace. Once again, she was perplexed at how I could be so calm and confident. Even if I could find the words to explain my journey into the Ethereal, there was no time left. All I could do was comfort her.

At 2:00 a.m. Bill came back into the room, nurses tagging behind him. It was time for surgery. I was wheeled down the long, white, sterile hallway that leads to the surgical suite, with Bill and Melanie on either side of the gurney. The nurse stopped short of the door and they could go no further. Bill assured me it was going to be OK and stepped away, giving me and Melanie a final moment together.

Melanie leaned over the gurney, staring through me with swollen eyes, desperately searching for an answer.

"Please tell me this won't be the last time I see you?"

"It's all good, Melanie. I assure you—I'll see you soon."

Once again the double doors of the surgical suite slowly opened and I could feel cool, purified air roll across my body. I heard the squeaking wheels of the gurney rolling me in slow motion toward the center of the room. This time my body was relaxed—ready to receive its gift.

JUNE 2016

IT'S NOT HOME ANYMORE

Four blurry days had passed since transplant, and I was out of intensive care, with a different team of nurses. I was coming out of the fog, lying in bed, and I felt a sensation, a constant push-pull motion as if I was being rocked in a cradle. I held onto my bed rails to see if I could stop it, but the rhythm continued. I had never felt anything like it.

At first I thought it was the pain medication playing mind tricks on me. I closed my eyes and breathed slowly to calm myself down. With my eyes closed I heard a sound that I recognized: lub-Dub, lub-Dub, lub-Dub... only this time it was faster and stronger than ever before. My eyes sprung open—my first reaction was panic. *Oh my God, someone else is living inside of me. This is so unnatural. What have I done!"*

The heartbeat was so strong it demanded all my attention. The more I focussed on it, the more it consumed me. I was frightened by feelings of being possessed by another human being. I had no idea I would feel this way. How could I? My mind couldn't process what was happening. Logic has no place here. Science found a way to put one human being inside another— it's beyond comprehension.

While a nurse tended to my various needs, a doctor I had never seen before entered my room.

"How are you feeling?" he asked.

"Doc," I responded anxiously, "who have they put inside me? The heartbeat is so strong, I feel like I'm going to be pushed out of my bed while I'm asleep. I have to hold onto the rails, because with each beat it feels like I'm being nudged closer to the edge."

"We put a Jaguar heart in you, kid," he said with a straight, expressionless face.

"No, seriously, Doc. Tell me."

He simply winked and walked out of my room.

"Who was that doctor?" I asked the attending nurse. "Is he part of the transplant team?"

"Everyone just calls him Dr. O. He's the doctor that goes out anytime of day or night and brings the hearts back. A heart can only live outside the body for four hours, so he's always on call. He's kind of mysterious, you know, because he's not allowed to tell us anything."

"Where is Dr. Uriel?" I asked anxiously. "I need to talk with him. I have a lot of questions."

"Dr. Uriel is with other patients and typically waits until you're a little further along in recovery to check on you. This is a step-down unit. You're with us the next few days, but Dr. O will check on you tomorrow. Get some rest."

The next day, Dr. O came into my room to check on me. I began my line of questioning before he had a chance to open his mouth.

"Doc, please tell me who you put inside me. This heart feels like it's pounding out of my chest. No one told me what to expect after transplant. Is this normal? I don't know how to feel. I'm freaking out! Would someone please talk to me?!"

Dr. O responded dispassionately, as if he was teaching a science class.

"First of all, I can't tell you anything about the donor, nor can anyone else. Fact is, you may never know about the donor. After one year, you can write a letter to the donor family through the organ donation agency, but they may or may not respond. Here's what I *can* tell you. After transplant, the donor heart knows it's no longer in its natural body, so it hesitates to start beating–"

I interrupted, "What do you mean it *knows* that it's not in its own body?"

"The heart contains its own system of neurons that rival the brain. The heart's neural networks interact with the brain, *imprinting* and storing many of our personality traits and preferences. In other words, the heart has a brain of its own."

"Wait, wait, wait, Doc. Are you telling me *the person* comes with the heart?!"

"To some degree, yes, but each patient is different. Only time will tell if some of the donor traits will express themselves. Anyway, since the heart has a brain of its own, it hesitates to start beating in a different body. So we must jumpstart the heart, so to speak, with medication the first few days after transplant to encourage it to beat. Yours was a rare case, however."

I stared at Dr. O, unsure I wanted to know the answer. But I had to.

"How so?" I asked him.

117

His poker face gave way to a childlike smirk.

"When we put your heart in, it took off running straight away. Whoever it is likes its new home."

Over the next several days, physical therapists walked me twice a day and taught me how to move my body without splitting my chest open. I had been preoccupied dealing with the pain of being sewn up like a Thanksgiving turkey, my sternum sawed open and wired back together. Right now, this body needed all of my attention. Even if I wanted to ignore my body's needs, my new companion, with its constant pounding in my chest, won't let me forget that *we* have a mission.

We? I couldn't shake the conversation I had with Dr. O a few days ago. *How much of this heart living inside me will express itself? What will become of me, in the "we?"* The thought that another person's imprint was encapsulated inside me was both frightening and fantastical. When I closed my eyes I could visualize my blood passing through the heart—our blood and DNA mixing together, our bodies becoming one. It's more than that. It felt as if the essence of this other person was with me now. This heart spoke to me. Each beat pounded in my ears. It was the sound of life, and it wanted to be heard. *Who are you?*

Whoever you are, I welcome you. I'm grateful for your gift of life, and in return I'll honor you by caring for my body. I'll be a good steward of your heart by not eating or drinking anything that might harm you. You are safe here. You are loved here. Make yourself at home.

On Tuesday June 14th, I was transferred back to the original room where my Chicago journey began. Coming full circle, recovering in the same room as before, I was having a *Wizard of Oz*/Dorothy moment. I'm back in Kansas all right. The pain in my body was a constant reminder of that. On the outside everything looked the same, but on the inside it felt like everything had changed.

And speaking of Oz, why was I not shown the *real* great and powerful Oz in the Ethereal? Isn't that what people think God is? The One and Only God of the Universe, Creator of All, standing by to answer prayers? The curtain was pulled back, the veil lifted for who knows how long? A millisecond, a nanosecond, a minute, eternity? In that time I did not meet the God I had come to believe in through my religious upbringing. In fact, I did not see any celestial beings. Instead, I was shown concepts and the framework behind Divine Intelligence.

Now my body was back home, but my spirit longed to return to the Ethereal. It felt as if I was floating between two worlds, my spirit wanting to free itself from this delicate vessel. If only I could have more time in that higher realm to ask questions, search for clues. I was told to testify, but how? I had more questions than answers.

My belongings still hung in the closet and, most importantly, my journal was tucked away on the bottom shelf. Dr. Uriel stopped by to visit. I was awestruck by our conversation and opened my journal as soon as he left the room.

Nir told me that as my heart was being removed during surgery, the main artery collapsed behind the two stents that Dr. Bajwa put in the night of my heart attack. Had my heart not been removed at that moment, I would have gone into cardiogenic shock and died. I asked him what time I received my new heart, and he told me it was 2:20 – 2:35 a.m., the same time of night my mother passed, as I placed that last drop of morphine under her tongue.

There were no words left to write in my journal. Even if I could find the words, the aphorism at the bottom of the page was enough to give me pause for the rest of my life. It confirmed what I have come to believe during this journey—that coincidences are God's way of remaining anonymous.

I will never fail you. I will never abandon you.

—Heb. 13:5

Although I was still processing the gamut of feelings and emotions, this was a time of celebration. I'm alive! I made it through unimaginable setbacks and circumstances beyond my control. It was the moment we have all worked toward—doctors, nurses, family, and friends—and the outcome could not have been better. Each of them contributed. Each brought to bear their own unique gift that culminated in this miraculous moment.

Geraldine strided into my room, beaming like a proud coach who just watched her student win an Olympic gold medal. Johnny, the ICU nurse that befriended me along the way, was tagging behind her. When I looked the most haggard and disheveled, Johnny helped restore my dignity by giving me a haircut with a tiny pair of stainless steel surgical scissors. I tucked those scissors away in my toiletry bag for keepsake. They're a symbol of thoughtful love extended by so many.

On several occasions, Lou and Carol brought homemade Italian food all the way from Pittsburgh to feed my caregivers. Lou inherited the mantle of leadership for the family at a very young age when our father died. No one would have faulted him for walking away from that responsibility. Instead, he picked it up and became our family's patriarch. Once again he took the lead, providing a foundation of support through my medical crisis.

The nurses loved coming into my room. It became an oasis, a place where all were welcome. They could easily feel the warmth and sense of family there. They also came to know Bill, who spent a great deal of time commuting from his home in Washington, DC along with his wife, Esther, to support me. They all sacrificed a great deal since that cold January night when this inexplicable journey began. There are no words to express my gratitude, for all the love and support my wife, family, and friends have given me freely.

I was overwhelmed by the love I felt at that moment. In between visits I turned to my journal to express some thoughts:

I see how God works through people. The only way God experiences life is through us. These acts offer proof that Spirit is intimately involved in our lives. It's the perfect system, letting us know God is always there, but still allowing us free will to act or not.

With each passing day, another drainage tube, the catheter, bandages, and IV's were removed. I felt like a time traveler in a science fiction movie, coming out of a cryogenic freeze. The time capsule had been opened, my heart was not my own, and my body was weak and atrophied from the journey. I'd returned to Earth, having traveled through another space-time dimension with knowledge to share. I felt like an alien in more ways than one. I also realized this was the time to rebuild my body.

I had not forgotten my promise to my niece, Teresa, and I was ready for a victory jog down the halls of the cardiac floor. Friends gathered outside my room, waiting to cheer me on. Determined to pull this off, I approached the closet and took the Rocky robe off its hanger. I played the *Rocky* soundtrack over and over in my head as I suited up, attempting to coax an adrenaline rush in my mind to help ease the pain in my body. I placed the cotton mask on my face (required whenever I leave my room), and down the hall I went. My sister-in-law, Esther, was behind me video-taping the escapade.

With every step I felt my skin stretching and pulling on the sutures, especially when I put my hands above my head to emulate my victory dance. The jog was slow, to say the least, my breath short, and pain radiated from every freshly sewn-up piece of flesh.

Teresa was right, it is a meaningful and gratifying moment for the nurses and doctors who have chosen this profession. The halls filled with laughter and joy. Everyone clapped and cheered as I passed. Patients lying in bed lifted their heads off pillows, enjoying a medical comrade's hopeful moment. I managed to jog into the ICU, giving a high-five to Dr. O, who didn't recognize me, masked under that big red hood. The security guard at the end of the hall saw me coming and shouted, "Go for it, Rocky!"

The video clip went viral. Teresa shared it with the medical team that she works with in Pittsburgh, where it became a source of inspiration. Unbeknownst to me, Lou sent the clip to doctors Bajwa, Patel, and Carson back in North Carolina. They were still with me on this journey.

Now that I was transplanted, I had to live up to my end of the deal that I made with Dr. Uriel, when he agreed to take me on as a patient. For one full year, I had to live near the hospital to be monitored. The risk of the donor heart rejecting its new home was the highest in the first year, requiring regular heart biopsies. Behind the scenes, Lou and Bill searched out and found an apartment in nearby Forest Park, IL. Once again, Lou took the lead and hauled furnishings from Pittsburgh.

On June 24th, 2016, sixteen days after transplant, a doctor from the transplant team came into my room with my release papers. Melanie was there, along with my work friend, Ali, to help me gather my belongings. Separation anxiety began to set in. It was hard to leave those who cared for me, but I knew they would always be with me. I was thankful Geraldine and Johnny were off on the day of my release, making it easier for me to leave.

As we finished loading my belongings into Ali's car, the ICU security guard happened to be walking by the main hospital entrance. He enthusiastically raised his fisted hands over his head, shouting out a final farewell: "Good luck, Rocky!"

In the back of Ali's car with Melanie, on the drive to my apartment, I hoped the ride wouldn't end. I needed time to process my thoughts and feelings. Something had shifted inside me, and it was more than just my perspective on life. It was a foundational shift, to the core of my being. My journey into the Ethereal was *the* experience that every religious or spiritual person prays for and hopes to obtain—that moment when the veil is pulled back just far enough to realize, without question, that God exists.

I felt trapped between two worlds, craving my true home in the Ethereal, and realizing that I had a task to complete. Yet all I wanted to do was get back to that place of unity and peace.

How could I possibly feel this way? How selfish and ungrateful can I be? After all the sacrifices family and friends made, support from my employer, the marvelous, dedicated people who helped save my life along the way? I've experienced miracle after miracle, yet all I want to do is retreat back into the spirit world. Am I a coward?

Ali's car hit a pothole and sent a jolting pain to my chest from wounds still tender from surgery. This snapped me out of my daydream and reminded me I was very much living in the physical world. Ali pulled up to the curb in front of the apartment and I was frozen in the back seat, reluctant to move. Any movement sent breathtaking waves of pain across my chest. I felt like a freshly-carved pumpkin in more ways than one. My insides had been removed, and in their place, a stranger resided.

"Just stay here and rest," Melanie said, turning around in her seat, "until Ali and I unload everything into the apartment." I was relieved.

While they unloaded the car, I realized I was stalling, using the pain in my body as an excuse to delay the mission before me. My mind went back to five months ago when I first came out of my coma and Pastor Eric came to visit from the Lutheran church in Cherryville. I felt the same now as I did then; frail, weak, and uncertain what the future held.

Now I remember what he said: *"People of great faith are also people of doubt."*

Looking back over these past months I realize now that faith got me this far. Faith that, no matter what happened next in my life, circumstances would somehow work out for my own good.

Melanie tapped on the car window.

"Okay, love," she said, "everything is unloaded. Let me help you out of the car."

Standing on the sidewalk, saying goodbye to our friend Ali, it was a beautiful, crystal-clear Chicago day. My feet were on the ground, someone else's heart was pumping blood through my veins, and my spirit still glimmered with stardust from the journey—longing to return home. I simultaneously cried tears of sadness and joy. I was happy to be alive and with Melanie again, but missing the peace and freedom of the Ethereal. I no longer knew where I belonged.

We turned toward the apartment and up the four wooden steps I went, holding onto the rail like a wizened old man. My weak, atrophied body shook, and I envisioned each leg muscle working like a set of pulleys, struggling to raise my legs up the next step. I was reminded again what an incredible machine I have been given to carry my spirit around while on earth. It must be cared for and nurtured; but much like wrapping paper on a gift, discarded when spirit transcends into the Ethereal.

Once in the apartment, I headed straight to the shower. For almost three months, I had only been able to take sponge baths and have my hair washed with a dry chemical mix inside a plastic shower cap. I raised my face toward the shower head, as if staring up at the sky, and dropped my arms to my sides. Warm water caressed my body, washing away the last remnants of my hospital stay.

I lost track of time, relishing the moment, until Melanie knocked on the door.

"Hey, you okay? You've been in there a long time."

"Yeah, I'm fine," I replied reluctantly, not wanting to move. I stayed in the shower until there was no hot water left to comfort me, and the oncoming cold water forced me out of my comfort zone. I realize why I didn't want it to end. This was no ordinary shower. This was my baptism back into a world that I no longer wanted to be part of, but must. This world pales in comparison to the beauty, love, and oneness of the Ethereal.

I had to remind myself, *there is more work to be done, a task given you to complete, you cannot return until your purpose is fulfilled.* These thoughts gave me the strength to push through the physical pain in my body, the emotional pain of being separated from Melanie and Maria, and the longing to return to my true home.

I stepped out of the tub, and, reaching for a towel to dry myself, I saw a reflection in the mirror of an unrecognizable figure. Sadness and empathy overwhelmed me as I stared at my scarred and atrophied body. The longer I gazed and overcame the initial shock, the more I remembered that my physical appearance was not the best part of me—a lesson I learned in the Ethereal.

I wept, not out of vanity, but of time wasted, focused too much on my outward appearance rather than my true life within. Somewhere deep inside me, I knew this to be the truth, long before my spiritual awakening.

How did I get lost along the way? What distractions could have derailed me to lose focus on the only real power in the world—the Divine within?

Melanie burst through the bathroom door.

"Rob, seriously, do you realize how long you have been in here? What's the matter? You look like you just saw a ghost"

"I did," I told her with a sly smile. "A ghost of what was and what could be."

"Okay, that makes no sense," she said, fishing for further information.

"I can't explain it yet," I told her. "I'm trying to make sense of it myself. It's my first day back in the world, and I'm really tired. Let's just eat dinner, Okay?"

During dinner Melanie brought me up to speed on what's been happening back home, but only part of me heard her. I was sitting at the table, but I wasn't really there. My thoughts vacillated between the physical and spiritual. When I focused on the physical, I was overwhelmed by the pain in my body, and when I shifted back to thoughts of the Ethereal, the pain subsided. I detached and it seemed like I was hovering outside myself.

I heard a name that sent me plummeting back to Earth—Maria.

"I'm sorry, Melanie, what did you say?"

She had no sense that I'd been absent from the conversation and she started over.

"I was saying how miraculous it's been that Maria hasn't had any seizures since you've been gone. Even the caregivers found it strange how stable she's been in your absence. We all thought the reverse would have been true. We thought we'd be living in the hospital like we've been doing for so long."

Something clicked and I lit up.

"Of course, Melanie!"

She stared at me, bewildered.

"Maria is the lynchpin that can help me explain that part of my experience. She's pure in spirit and there have been many times when she has used circumstances to speak to us. I understand that now! I need to go back through my journals and tie these experiences together."

I realized I had detached from the conversation again when Melanie told me that she'd bring my other journals on her next trip here. Her words were warm, but she looked forlorn.

"I'm sorry, Melanie," I told her.

She straightened her posture, minding her manners as if she just remembered she was at a formal dinner. Suddenly I was struck with the feeling that the dining room chairs felt foreign to me. Everything did. Normal was a lifetime ago. It no longer existed.

"I know you have needs too," I told her. "You must feel so neglected. We have a lot to catch up on. We've been through hell."

She nodded.

"I don't know how to explain what's happening to me," I continued. "The world seems different to me now, and I'm having a hard time fitting back in. Even with you sitting right here I feel alone… I know you're lonely too, though."

She closed her eyes and put her hand on top of mine. She wanted me to continue.

"You know that phrase, 'To be *in* the world, but not *of* it?' I'm trying to figure that out."

I stopped short of telling her that the kind of loneliness I was experiencing was strange and otherworldly, but I think she sensed it anyway.

"Rob, you just had a heart transplant; this is your first day back in the world. I understand why you would feel that way. Look, you have a year to journal and get your head together, but right now, you need to focus on Dr. Uriel's instructions, remember? Every day, all he wants you to do is walk, rest, walk, rest, and let your body heal. Lou arrives when I leave Sunday morning, so let's just try and enjoy these two days together... OK?"

Watching Melanie roll away in the taxicab Sunday morning, I realized how difficult it was going to be for others to relate to me. I sensed an emptiness, and I could feel Melanie's pain as she realized there was a part of me she couldn't reach.

The curious thing was that I felt more connected to her and others at a much deeper level than ever before, because now I knew where we came from. I knew we were all connected in spirit and of the same source. I couldn't find the words to describe this oxymoron. How could I feel more connected to others and at the same time feel so alone? I now understood why I wasn't pining away for Maria's touch. We had always spoken in spirit, and she responded in the physical. She understands the silent language of the unseen world better than anyone. Although I had missed her and longed to hold her, I was closer to her now in spirit than ever before. I could only get so close, as the spirit connects at a much deeper level.

More than ever, I felt the pressure to articulate my experience. I wanted the whole world to see the beauty in others beyond the flesh, to make known what I had been searching for all along in my relationship with Maria. It's the same thing we all need—to know we are loved at the core of our being. When she spoke those words in the

> IT'S THE SAME THING WE ALL NEED—TO KNOW WE ARE LOVED AT THE CORE OF OUR BEING.

Ethereal—*Just love me*—I had an awareness she was not just inferring to love her, the person, but rather the source of love that connects and binds us all together as one. The light I saw beaming through her eyes was the same light I saw in the web.

The more I loved, the more the light spread. The more it spread, the closer I became to God.

I took a seat on the front porch, outside, where I felt most connected to the universe. I waited for Lou to arrive. I couldn't be alone for the first three months, so he'd arranged a rotation schedule of family and friends to stay with me.

My dinner table conversation with Melanie on the subject of love triggered a long-forgotten memory. In the summer of 2011 Maria had just been through five days of seizures. We were all strung out and exhausted after living in the hospital. We came home, put Maria to bed, and, to get our mind off things, decided to watch a Stephen Hawking documentary on his theory of the universe. It was my first exposure to his ideas, and the way the film used examples to explain the complexities of physics were both fascinating and simple to understand.

Hawking's theory was that the universe was created from the Big Bang, which came out of a black hole. Inside the black hole time stands still, so there was no time for God to be created, therefore God does not exist. After what we had been through with Maria for five days, I was silently considering Hawking's theory in my mind. After the film, I turned out the light and drifted off to sleep.

Then out of the darkness, I heard Melanie say "Then where did love come from?"

"Go to sleep, hun. We'll talk tomorrow."

"How can love come out of a black hole?" Melanie insisted. "Even if I were an evolutionist, it still doesn't explain how love could evolve. How can something evolve if it doesn't exist in the first place? Where does our moral compass come from, our innate sense of right and wrong? Where else can that come from except a loving God?"

"Are you talking to yourself or trying to convince me?" I replied with my back facing her.

Melanie sat up in the bed.

"Both! Love had to come from somewhere. It can't evolve if it doesn't exist. One can't exist without the other. No God, no love. No love, no God. It's a self-fulfilling prophecy—don't you see?!"

"You make a good point, Melanie. I wish it were that simple. Let's talk in the morning, okay?"

I rolled over, remaining silent until she fell asleep, not wanting her to know that her words gave me great pause. My cell phone rang, reminding me I was sitting on the front porch of my apartment in Chicago. Lou's voice was enthusiastic.

"Brother Rob, I'm ten minutes away," he said. "Put your walking shoes on."

While waiting for him to arrive, I recalled the morning I left for Chicago. With her eyes Maria gave me permission to come here, and then her body cooperated. She has been trying to show me all along how the Ethereal operates in the physical realm. Love—conveyed through strong emotional feelings—replaces the spoken word and expresses her thoughts more succinctly.

These past twenty years I have mourned not being able to hear her voice. At times I have been driven to the brink of madness, carrying on a one-way conversation, replacing what I hoped were her words, with my own—even parroting them aloud. Many nights I dreamed that she spoke to me. I'd run into her room filled with hope once she awoke, only to be deflated again when she remained silent. Having seen her in the Ethereal, I remember what she said: *Just love me.*

I thought, *Love is the Universal language God uses to speak through all of creation.*

I pulled out my journal and scribbled some thoughts before Lou arrived:

June 26, 2016

> *How am I going to explain what I encountered? I'm not a physicist or religious scholar. The word "God" carries many different meanings. Different religious beliefs create separation, yet all I experienced was unity. My encounter with divine intelligence directly conflicts with the belief system that I was raised with and had come to expect. What I experienced was "that simple" in the Ethereal, but complex in the physical.*

Walking the first mile on the streets of Forest Park with Lou, I was forced to use every ounce of mental and physical energy just to take the next step.

"Are you OK?" he kept asking.

I was calling on my spirit to float above the scene like a kite, more hopeful than ever that I could return to the Ethereal on command. Then I heard a loud screeching police car and my spirit came crashing back to the ground. The pain in my body returned, along with the disappointment that I could only ascend so far.

LOVE IS THE UNIVERSAL LANGUAGE GOD USES TO SPEAK THROUGH ALL OF CREATION.

Lou turned to face me.

"Are you ready to turn back?"

"No, I'm not ready to give up yet," I said. I couldn't tell him it wasn't about the walk. It was about wanting to return to the Ethereal.

Over the next three months, it was wonderful to reconnect with various family members and friends as they came to visit, each helping me in their own way through this fragile period.

I found myself wanting to share some of the details of my experience, but I knew I would be misunderstood. While engaging in conversation, my mind constantly wandered. I felt I didn't relate to the world, especially when someone turned on the news.

The U.S. presidential election was in full swing and I was appalled by the degrading nature of the campaign tactics. It was painful to watch human beings strip away each other's dignity instead of working together for the common good. The country was reeling from a June 12th attack by a twenty-nine-year-old male at a gay night club in Orlando, that killed forty-nine people and left another fifty-three wounded. In July, a racially motivated sniper killed five police officers in Dallas, Texas. The civil war in Syria was decimating the country and slaughtering thousands of civilians. North Korea continued to conduct missile and nuclear tests. Brazil and South Korea impeached their presidents on corruption charges, while Russia was accused of interfering with U.S. elections.

Coming back into the world, I saw division, dissension, and hatred. When I focused on the spiritual realm, it felt like I was standing in the eye of a hurricane where it's calm and safe. Grappling with the incongruence between the two worlds was both motivating and depressing. I knew if I didn't reconcile this, I would not be able to fulfill my purpose.

I remembered again when I first met Dr. Jeevenandum. He floated into my hospital room and asked what I had learned. I told him "I can't control anything."

Control.

I've been shown time and time again, that when I let go and trust, everything works out for good. The Rev told me long ago, "God can't take control, until you relinquish control." So why am I having such a hard time letting go?

My journaling was sporadic during the three months of visitations. Dealing with the constant needs of my body—medication changes, restricted diet, follow-up testing at the hospital—it was all consuming. I knew on a spiritual level that everything I had been shown in the Ethereal was true, but still, I couldn't seem to find my way forward to accept that I was back in the world. Seeing the world with fresh eyes makes it all the more difficult to be here.

Late September rolled around quickly, and I was finally on my own. It was time to dig deep; to go within and try to make sense of it all.

Secretly, I convinced myself that I would find a way to get back to that place of peace and unity. Somehow I would find a way to escape this horrifying new world and climb the ladder back to the Ethereal.

To this end, every morning I went through a prayer and meditation routine. For hours, I projected my mind back into that infinite expanse, trying desperately to ascend. When I open my eyes, I am disappointed to discover gravity holding me down on my bed. I was becoming increasingly frustrated at not being able to reconcile the spiritual world, where I longed to return, with the physical world where I must live. Quietly I was becoming more depressed.

On a pleasant Sunday morning, my boss called.

"I would like you to meet my pastor from the Chinese American Church I attend," he told me. "It's not far from your apartment. Can we stop by after service this morning?"

"I don't know Paul," I told him. "What kind of church is it, and does this guy speak English?"

He laughed.

"It's nondenominational," he told me, "and Pastor Man speaks English well enough for you to understand. We'll be there shortly."

It was a crisp, sunny day, and the smell of fall drifted through the air. I was sitting at the table on the front porch when they pulled up to the curb. Pastor Man has straight black hair with a tint of gray, smooth skin, and dark eyes hiding behind his glasses. His demeanor is cheerful, smiling from ear to ear as he bounced briskly up the steps and introduced himself.

"I'm Pastor Man," he said with exuberance, while simultaneously extending his hand and bowing with respect.

Sensing we needed privacy, Paul went inside and waited patiently.

Pastor Man took a seat next to me, and folded his hands in front of him, resting on the table. He smiled, staring straight through me, but said nothing. I stared back, lifting my eyebrows, encouraging him with my facial expressions to speak first. He just kept smiling, baiting me to make the first move. It felt like a chess game. The longer we played, the more emotional I got. My eyes become glossy with tears, and my body language telegraphed everything he needed to know. I was desperate to let it out, but unsure I could trust him.

Should I move my pawn, giving him just enough information to see how he reacts, or move my king into checkmate—risking it all by telling him how I really feel? He may think I'm crazy. What if he tells Paul I've lost my mind and I'm no longer employable? Wait, don't you remember—let go...

Something in my spirit told me I was safe, so I decided to move my king into checkmate.

"I don't know where to start," I told him. "I feel so guilty that I got a heart, while so many others will die waiting for a heart that may never come. Kids, young people who have their whole lives in front of them... why me?"

I paused to wipe my face and catch my breath. Pastor Man was still smiling.

"What makes it even worse is, I don't even want to be here. Can you imagine dealing with that?! And this will make absolutely no sense to you... I'm grateful to be alive, but having caught a glimpse of the spirit world, I don't want to be here. I know I was sent back with a purpose and to take care of my family, but the truth is, I don't know where I belong."

Pastor Man broke his gaze for the first time since he sat down, and stared out into the street, leaving me in suspense. After a moment, he turned back to look at me with a softer smile.

"The solution to your problem is very simple," he replied with confidence. "You don't know where you belong yet, because you are fat in the spirit, having been fed too much during your spiritual journey. To get thin again, give back to God by serving others in all your works. The divine nature will express itself more fully through the gifts of the spirit—kindness, faith, goodness, forgiveness, respect, and love. Serving others will also take away any guilt about getting a heart. You don't have to leave the earth to experience the Divine."

Paul walked out onto the porch.

"You guys had enough time?"

"Plenty of time, Paul. Thank you for bringing Pastor Man," I told him, as we stood to say our goodbyes.

"Come to our church when you're ready," Pastor Man invited. We have a Pastor for our English congregation—you'll like him. I hope to see you again."

As Paul pulled away from the curb, I locked the apartment door behind me and walked. The first mile is always the hardest, and I called on my spirit once again, to lift me up and out of the scene. But something changed—my feet were still on the pavement. Pastor Man's words felt like weights on a hot air balloon. The more I contemplated them, the more grounded I became, forcing me to accept my new reality. The further I walked, the more I noticed myself becoming increasingly connected to my surroundings. I recalled the last thing he said to me: "You don't have to leave the Earth to experience the Divine."

"YOU DON'T HAVE TO LEAVE THE EARTH TO EXPERIENCE THE DIVINE."

Something compelled me to stop on the sidewalk and pluck a large leaf, the size of my hand, from a low-hanging branch of an oak tree. I tore the leaf in half with reverence, from tip to stem, placing one half in each hand as I closed my eyes and took in a deep breath while gently squeezing the leaf. I could feel the life energy of the leaf flowing into my body and giving me strength.

Just then I recall a memory. When I was thirteen years old, I took karate lessons at the prompting of my older brothers. I was a scrawny kid, constantly getting bullied because I didn't fit in anywhere. Being raised in a rough-and-tumble steel town where brawn and might were celebrated, I possessed neither—I was a misfit. I struggled with the physical aspect of karate, so when I jogged alone as part of the training, I would stop along the path in the woods and pull leaves off trees, squeezing them with all my might, asking them to share their energy. When I finished jogging, I would release the shriveled leaves, thanking them for their companionship and energy as they fell to the ground in front of me—a secret I could never share.

I have always felt most wholly like myself when immersed in nature. I had lost sight of the divine in everything, but now I was rediscovering, from a holistic perspective, the divine that surrounds me. When I saw the web in the Ethereal, I experienced the interconnectedness of everything and the web awakened a deeper understanding inside me.

WHEN I SAW THE WEB IN THE ETHEREAL, I EXPERIENCED THE INTERCONNECTEDNESS OF EVERYTHING AND THE WEB AWAKENED A DEEPER UNDERSTANDING INSIDE ME.

I opened my hands to look at the leaf, and it was almost as if I had X-ray vision, seeing the leaf for what it really is, examining its design and not just looking at it.

Could this leaf be a microcosm of the web I saw in the Ethereal? Unwittingly, as a lonely, thirteen-year-old misfit, could I have been trying to draw strength from nature? Can this leaf be a piece to the puzzle?

I dropped the leaf to the ground, and thanked it for sharing itself with me, just like I did in the woods all those years ago. I galloped back to my apartment—at least it felt like a gallop to me—ignoring the pain in my body. I couldn't get the key into the lock fast enough, leaving the door wide open behind me as I rushed over to my computer and Googled, "anatomy of a leaf."

I'm struck by the similarities in design, at a cellular level, between the leaf, an animal, and a human being. I dig deeper, into the molecular level, then even deeper into the atomic level—and then I see an image that transports me back into the Ethereal.

The mechanism is the same for both animate and inanimate objects. Same design—atom, nucleus, surrounded by rotating electrons, just on different scales. It doesn't matter if it's a leaf, cerebral cortex of the brain, or the solar system. Could this be the meaning of one of the concepts expressed to me in the Ethereal: "I Am the origin of all?"

My experience with the leaf reconnected me to the Ethereal more profoundly than the hours I spent trying to ascend in prayer and meditation. As I began to see the divine all around me, fragments of the concepts I was shown streamed into my awareness. As the days passed, messages came to me, but I felt stuck until a friend drove me to an office supply store where I was drawn to huge sheets of self-stick poster paper that sat on an easel.

Now when a thought comes to me, I rush over with my magic marker and write it down. I fill a page, then tear it from the easel and post it on the wall. Then I start on the next blank sheet. By late October, messages had fallen out of me like leaves on the trees outside my window. The more I opened my spirit, the more I received, and sometimes the messages came to me in dreams. One morning I was sipping coffee before sunrise, and I sensed the familiar unspoken voice of the Ethereal:

When there is no way out… go within. That's where you'll find true security and the root of all fear. There you'll find your real identity, intrinsic value, and the power of a single act.

I had been praying to remember some of the details from my journey into the Ethereal, but instead of feeling relief, I felt fear. These statements came to me as brand-new insights, rather than answers; pieces to a bigger puzzle which I was now responsible for putting together. Where did the phrase "The power of a single act" come from, and how did that relate to my experience? Once again, I felt immense pressure to figure this out, and anxiety rising within me, so I called the Rev and read him the messages on my posters.

"Rev, you see what I'm talking about now? I don't know what's happening to me. These thoughts are coming to me in bits and pieces. Some I can relate to as I look back through my journal notes, but others make no sense at all. Do you think my mind is playing tricks on me?"

"Not at all," he assured me. God speaks to us through circumstances in our lives and through dreams. You have had a profound spiritual experience and your door has been opened. Don't shut it now. Don't be afraid. Let the holy spirit speak freely through you. The more you remain open, the more you will receive when you're ready to handle it—that's how God's timing works. Did you know that Albert Einstein's theory of relativity was inspired by a dream?"

WHEN WE REMAIN IN SPIRIT, KNOWLEDGE FLOWS THROUGH US, NEVER FROM US. SPIRIT IS THE CONDUIT THROUGH WHICH ALL KNOWLEDGE IS REVEALED.

"What?" I asked.

"Look it up. Research all these things, now that you the time. Many of the great minds and prophets throughou history, and even today, have been inspired through dreams. Remember, the Latin root word for *inspired* is, 'in spirit.' When we remain in spirit, knowledge flows through us, never from us. Spirit is the conduit through which all knowledge is revealed."

"That makes sense, Rev," I told him, now feeling a bit lighter. "That helps explain part of my experience in the Ethereal when the awareness came to me that, *'All I have to do is observe and any question is already answered.'*"

"Yes!" the Rev replied, "this is how you hear the voice of God in the temporal world."

"But I'm afraid to let more come through me," I said. "Afraid I'll be misunderstood, I guess. I'm most afraid of receiving more knowledge and not being able to live up to it in the *real* world. I keep telling myself to keep the faith. but–"

The Rev interrupted my tangent, and pulled me back from the edge.

"Faith and fear are the same thing. Faith is the belief that something good is going to happen. Fear is the belief that something bad is going to happen. How do you choose to live?"

Sitting on the living room couch, I had an epiphany. In my mind's eye, I imagined the ceiling retracting like a car's sunroof, while the four walls surrounding me fell outwardly, crashing to the ground. I'm sitting in the middle of a white, open space. A youthful feeling surges through my body, as my spirit expands n feel myself smiling, because I've made

hen I hear the Rev's voice:

ill there?"

ve by faith," I told him. "I can't thank you

nded the call abruptly, feeling giddy as a child

on C.... orning—anticipating the unknown with joy.

With each passing day, the messages keep coming. They get more interesting and cryptic, prompting me to research each one separately as they pour out of me:

Everything in the universe is one: one God, one people, all made the same

Why is peace so difficult?

The brain does not create reality or consciousness

Consciousness exists; we receive and observe

Thanksgiving came and I was alone, trying to pretend it's just another day. A steel industry colleague of mine stopped by unexpectedly and offered to take me out for lunch. I was delighted to reconnect with an old friend and to get out of the apartment for a while. After a warm greeting in the foyer, I invited him in. As he entered the living room, I sensed an immediate shift in his energy. His eyes darted around the room like a scanner.

"Make yourself at home, Kevin," I told him. "It won't take me a minute to get dressed." I didn't give a second thought to the posters hanging on my living room walls. While getting dressed, the start-stop creaking sound of the hardwood floor outside my bedroom signaled Kevin's movements. A cold chill washed over me as he walked through the room, as if he were in a museum, stopping at each poster and soaking it in before he moved on to the next one.

I threw the rest of my clothes on and anxiously opened the bedroom door. He stared at me like I was a stranger, his eyebrows squeezed tightly together, right eyebrow raised, exaggerating the size of his right eye. His mouth was slightly open, his lower lip angling down to the left, in an awkward position. The silence between us was untenable, so I managed a sheepish smile to try and break it.

Kevin waved at one of the posters and let it all out.

"What the hell does that mean, the brain doesn't create reality?! I get up every day and bust my ass to create my own reality. Who's gonna create my reality if I don't... huh?!"

"Kevin, listen," I assured him, "these are just some thoughts–"

He interrupted angrily.

"No, you listen. You've had a break *from* reality, man, because you have too much time on your hands. You need to start working part-time and forget about this crap. People are going to think you're crazy!"

I'm not ready to talk about this yet. I need to get him out of here and put these away later.

"Come on, man, I've been through a lot this year," I explained. "I'm just going through some stuff, you know? Let's just go to lunch, okay? You can catch me up on what's been going on in the industry."

His face relaxed as he saw the familiar in me once again, and we headed out the door for lunch.

We walked to a restaurant a few blocks away and got seated. Kevin pulled out two cell phones and placed them on either side of his plate; personal cell phone on the left, business on the right.

He took in a deep breath and slowly let it out with a forced smile—I could see that he was feigning his presence in the moment. He folded his hands in front of him, rested them on the plate, and leaned in.

"So, how are you feeling?" he asked me.

"Physically I'm still feeling a bit fragile, but–"

His business phone rang.

"Sorry, I've got to take this," he said. "This guy's been trying to get me for days."

Before I could say a word, he's on the call. The waitress approached with our menus. She handed me mine but was uncertain what to do with his, as he was oblivious to her presence. I apologized for him.

"He'll be done shortly," I told her. "Just put it on his plate."

"Alright," he said into his cell phone before hanging up. "I'll send you an email confirmation right now."

He asked me to give him another minute while he conducted some more business. I nodded in agreement and our waitress returned.

"Have you guys decided?"

Kevin picked up his menu and blindly fumbled through the pages. Without much thought, he ordered a burger and fries, snapped his menu shut- all while typing on his cell phone and occasionally glancing up at me.

I rotated my water glass on the table, pretending I was also preoccupied, examining each section of the glass as I twirled it round and round like a carousel. Water droplets formed on the outside of the glass as the ice melted. I focused on each droplet, as if I was looking at them through a telescopic lens, delighting in each one as they splashed onto my fingers.

The droplets pull me into a meditative state, freeing my mind and allowing me to retreat into my own world. As I detached further from the scene, it felt like part daydream, part spiritual insight. The telescopic lens pulls back to wide-angle, opening up my view of the restaurant, like movie theater curtains pulled back on a screen. I realize Kevin is not the only one with his face buried in his cell phone — everyone in the restaurant seems to be doing the same.

It's filled with carbon copies of Kevin, displaying the same addictive behavior of junkies anesthetized with their digital fix. Businesspeople, friends, families with children, no one seems to be communicating directly with one another. I watched two young kids at the table next to us, sitting across from each other texting instead of talking, while simultaneously watching a movie on their phones. The parents are so preoccupied on their own phones they're missing the joy of childhood sitting right there at the table with them. No one even looks up to acknowledge the waitress—another luminous soul—as she sets their food in front of them. If they only knew what I would give to have a conversation with my Maria.

Where are the beautiful human beings I saw in the Ethereal that were filled with light? This feels like a dystopian future movie, or maybe it's a Truman Show-like unreal reality, where everything is staged. We are all here craving human touch, but even sitting across from one another we are still alone. Does this room represent a dim part of the web I saw in the Ethereal? I want to shout out to everyone, 'Can't you see you have gifts!?'

145

But I don't. Instead I warn myself to be careful as I return… in no time this could easily be me. Kevin entered back into the conversation abruptly, as if he never stopped talking.

"...anyway, good to see you again, man. I'm so glad you're doing well."

Constant disruptions from calls, texts, and emails continued during our entire meal. When he did take a moment to eat, he didn't chew, but gobbled huge chunks of his burger. I kept the conversation focused on business, in the hopes that he wouldn't bring up my posters again, but it didn't take long to realize that he's already forgotten them.

We walked back to the apartment and I was thankful Kevin had no time to come back in and visit. The first thing I did inside was carefully take down each poster, clip them together, and place them under my bed.

From now on when I fill a page, I will tear it from the easel and place it under the bed with the others. No one will see my thoughts again until I'm ready.

The lunch episode left me feeling uncertain about returning to the working world. I dread the thought of becoming so programmed and robotic, just going through the motions, working for a paycheck while giving little consideration to the real life within me.

I'm learning to see the Divine in everything again, but how can I strike a balance between the spiritual and physical worlds? How can I share my experience so that others can relate?

Christmas was coming, and I tried to keep thoughts of home at bay. There would be no sense of normalcy or wonder this year.

My monthly checkup with Dr. Uriel came the first week of December and I felt the usual nervousness at what the visit might bring... until he burst through the door.

"Rob, your heart is doing fantastic!" he told me. "There are no signs of rejection or infection. That's a critical milestone in the first six months. So..." He held back a warm smile filled with anticipation.

I could only remain silent for a few seconds... "OK Nir, tell me!"

"I'm going to let you fly home for Christmas," he said, "but you can only be away for four days."

"Give me five days, Nir, please?" I pleaded.

He shook his head no, but quickly conceded. "OK, fine. But only if you promise to wear your mask on the plane and constantly sanitize your hands. You have to wear the mask if anyone at home is sick."

"Deal!" I jumped off the examining table, thanking Nir with a hug and kiss on his cheek. In my excitement, I headed out the door.

"Wait... we're not done," he told me, taking on a serious tone. "Sit down, Rob. When you get back, we need to check your prostate cancer again. Your PSA has risen slightly since transplant. Having been on immune suppressants for six months now, I'm not surprised the cancer has spread a little more, but should it rise again, we'll have to remove the prostate. You remember our deal, right?"

"How could I ever forget?" My eyes drifted to the floor. "Don't get me wrong, Nir, I'm so grateful. It's just the thought of another surgery so early on and–"

147

"Hey," he interrupted, "look at me. You're alive! Go home and enjoy your family. We'll deal with this together when the time comes."

I responded with a warm smile, as he left the room—there's nothing more to say.

On the way back to my apartment, riding in the rear seat of a taxicab, different scenarios ran through my head in anticipation of going home. There was a sick feeling in my stomach, but it was from more than backseat car sickness, though the cab driver did weave through traffic like a snake running for its life. It occured to me now why I had resisted participating in live Skype calls with Maria over the past six months. Having seen her perfect and whole in the Ethereal, I had not yet been ready to see her struggling again inside her broken body.

Midmorning on December 21st, 2016, my plane touched down in Charlotte, North Carolina. Walking through the airport, I might as well have been invisible compared to what I experienced back in April, when I left for Chicago. I'm no longer a pale, ashen cyborg with lights flashing and pumps whirling. This time there are no judgmental stares to make me feel inadequate or less than human. For a fleeting moment, I'm relieved that I'm accepted again in society. Then I think of Maria and others like her, who spend their entire lives feeling, looking, and being treated differently.

I also had a sense of disappointment that nothing had changed in the world, until I saw Melanie waiting for me at the bottom of the escalator with arms wide open. She embraced me like a soldier's wife, whose husband returned from battle. Coming back to this airport for the first time, I was overwhelmed

148

with joy, and left my negative feelings behind—it was time to go home.

While Melanie drove us home, my mind focused on how Maria will react when she sees me again. In the past when I traveled for work, having been gone only several days at a time, Maria would express her anger with my absence by refusing to make eye contact with me. She would raise her nose in the air and turn her head to the right, not allowing me to enter her space—sometimes for hours.

As we pulled down the driveway, my donor heart pounded with anticipation. This would be the first time I set foot in my home since I left Maria's beside that cold April morning. I rushed into the house with Melanie trailing right behind me. Maria was at the kitchen table, having just finished the lunch her caregiver fed her. I stood in the doorway, waiting to see how she reacted before I took another step. She looked up at me, immediately making eye contact and allaying my fears.

I took a few steps toward her, and before I finished saying "Maria, it's Daddy" in a wobbly voice, I realized no words were even needed. Her eyes filled with light. Her face shined with that same knowing smile that I have seen so many times in our darkest physical moments, as well as that brightest spiritual moment while in the Ethereal. We instantly connected.

I knelt down in front of her, taking her hands in mine so she couldn't wring them, and placed our hands together in her lap.

Pastor Man's words come to mind... *"You don't have to leave the earth to experience the Divine."*

I whispered my secret to her. "I understand now—sorry it took me so long." It felt like we were the only two people in the room.

All I could hear was white noise until Maria's caregiver interrupted.

"She's smiling so hard I think her face is going to break," she told me. It's time for her nap, anyway."

"Come on, love," Melanie chimed in. "Let me show you what I've done to the house while you were gone. Nothing major. Just changed a few wall colors. We'll save the Christmas tree for last!"

I drew a long breath through my nose, delighting in the wonderful smell of a live Christmas tree. Holding Melanie in front of the tree, I felt more connected to her than ever before. The smell of pine, and the warm glow of the white tree lights tucked behind huge cotton snowballs, put me in a euphoric state. This is how it feels to be alive. I wanted it more than I have in a long, long time.

The next day, Maria and I cuddled up next to the fireplace in her leather recliner. To get into the holiday spirit, we watched my favorite Christmas movie, *Rudolph the Red-Nosed Reindeer*. The scene when Santa and Rudolph go to the Island of Misfit Toys to rescue them from exile triggers a deeply-seated childhood memory.

Having felt like a misfit as a child and all through high school, I eagerly anticipate the scene when Santa and Rudolph boldly deliver each toy into a home, where they are accepted and valued just as they are. The cowboy that rides an ostrich, instead of a horse. A bird that swims instead of flying—I relate to all of them.

I cradled Maria tighter during this scene, which staves off both old and new feelings of inadequacy. My heart is not my own; someone else lives inside me. Likewise, Maria can't walk, talk, or feed herself—we are both like Santa's rescued toys.

Neither of our parts fit together, yet, while my strong heart came from someone else, my body has adopted it and it has embraced its new home.

Tonight, Maria was safe in my arms. I glanced at her to see how she reacts to this scene, and I found her staring right through me. We communicated in a language unspoken—a language all our own.

Maria would continue helping me remember what I learned in the Ethereal. A

WE ARE SPIRITUAL BEINGS, LIVING INSIDE FRAGILE CLAY VESSELS. THERE ARE NO MISFITS. WE ARE ALL CHILDREN BORN OF THE SAME LIGHT.

peace settled over me like I have never felt before, and these words of truth came to my mind: *We are spiritual beings, living inside fragile clay vessels. There are no misfits. We are all children born of the same light.*

DECEMBER 2016

ALL ONE

S omething inside me was unsettled. While I was home during
Christmas, I made an appointment to see Dr. Bajwa. Ever
since it happened I wanted to know more about that night in
January when I flatlined. I also wanted to see doctors Patel and
Carson, to express gratitude for saving my life—but I only had
enough time to see Dr. Bajwa.

Sitting in his office waiting room, my spirit was overwhelmed
and surrounded by a feeling of collective despair. Most of the
patients there were middle-aged men, slumped in their chairs
and staring at the floor with expressionless faces. Their wives
sat next to them, flipping through magazines without really
looking, or nervously picking at their fingernails, as they waited
to see the doctor.

I connected with these men on a deep, spiritual level, both
feeling and absorbing their emotional and physical symptoms. I
could relate to what they must have been thinking, having sat in

their chairs many times before. I reflected on my own thoughts at the time.

What would become of me now? Who would care for my family if I didn't make it? Has my time been well spent?

Once again, feelings of urgency and inadequacy came over me.

How could I share my story in a way that can help these men? I want to free them from their fears. Maybe I should just jump up, stand in the middle of the room, and tell them what it's like in the Ethereal. Okay, that's a dumb idea...

A voice snapped me out of my daydream.

"Rob, come on back," a nurse said. "Dr. Bajwa will see you now."

She led me into an examination room where I waited some more. I remember what I said to Dr. Bajwa in late March, the last time I sat in this room: "My future looks grim huh, doc?"

"Your future is not grim Rob," he assured me with a pat on the shoulder.. "You just can't see it yet."

It was the last time I saw him before my abrupt departure to Chicago. The exam room door swung open and his nurse stepped aside so Dr. Bajwa could enter.

"I'll leave you two alone," she told us.

As Dr. Bajwa entered the room, I gently rose to my feet, arms by my side, palms open toward him, and ready to receive. The love in his eyes accepted my invitation and my mind flashed back to the first time I saw his face. I was lying in a hospital bed, just coming out of my coma. I clearly remember looking up at him and knowing that language wasn't even necessary, that all needed communication was in his eyes. They conveyed peace, understanding, and most importantly... love.

We met in the middle of the room and embraced. Before a word was spoken tears fell from my eyes, not just from gratitude, but the deep spiritual validation I felt in the Ethereal that we are all connected.

"Come, sit down," Dr. Bajwa said, handing me a tissue. "You've been through a lot."

"Sorry about that," I said, wiping my eyes. "It's just… I never properly thanked you for saving my life that night."

"I didn't save your life," he said, with that same loving smile I saw when I first came out of my coma. "God did."

I ask him to explain.

"I remember everything about that night," he said, as his eyes drifted toward the window. "Your heart stopped pumping for an extended period of time. Your organs started shutting down. Honestly… I didn't think you were going to make it. I did all that I could as a physician, but it was God that saved your life."

I gazed back at Dr. Bajwa, and something in my spirit opened up. I felt safe, so I took a chance and shared part of what happened, at least to the extent that I understood it.

"I had an experience in Chicago," I told him, "before my donor heart arrived."

Behind his wire-rimmed glasses, Dr. Bajwa raised his eyebrows, signaling that I should continue. Yet unspoken words spilled from my mouth as if waiting for their chance to be heard.

"I was taken up into a timeless place," I explained, "and became both part of, and connected to, a vast interactive web that binds us all. I experienced unity and oneness with all things. I realized that I was not my body, race, or religion, and that there is a common thread woven through all of us; A universal language spoken, that I believe is–"

"Love," he said with a glowing smile.

"Yes, love." I rested for a moment on the beauty of these words, then continued. "But there's something else I want to understand better. Even though I was raised a Christian, I did not see a Christlike figure. Instead, I experienced God through concepts and saw light in everyone. May I ask you a question about your religious belief? I mean... I don't know anything about Sikhism."

"Don't feel bad," he replied with a chuckle. "At least you're curious enough to ask. Most people just make assumptions about us. Sikhism was founded in northern India by Guru Nanak in the late eighteenth century. It was said that from a very young age, he was always thinking about God and helping the poor. At age eleven, he rebelled against the caste system, refusing to wear the sacred thread."

"So, he was a rebel like Christ, huh? Did he have any siblings?"

"There are similarities in how Jesus and Nanak began their ministries. He had one sister, Bibi Nanaki, who said of him, 'I saw the Light of God in Nanak at a very young age.'"

"You know, Dr. Bajwa," I said introspectively, "after the Ethereal, my mind is open to understanding other religious beliefs, because I see how big and all-inclusive God is. Please tell me how Nanak began his ministry."

He went on to explain how Nanak would rise early every morning, go out to bathe in the river, and pray to God. One day, at the age of thirty, he didn't return. Many people thought he had drowned in the river, but after three days, Nanak appeared, sitting alone in the village common. An old man from the village approached him and asked, "Where have you been all these days, Nanak?"

156

"Nowhere," he said. "Here. I was with God. Now I have a lot of work to do."

"Work for whom?" the man asked him. "For the Hindus or the Muslims?"

"There is no Hindu and no Muslim," he replied. "We are all sons of the one God."

I stared at Dr. Bajwa, more compelled than ever to learn about the different belief systems of everyone I have encountered on my journey, and how they relate to what I experienced in the Ethereal.

"What happened to Nanak after that?" I asked. "I mean, was he persecuted?"

"As you can imagine, he was ostracized from his village for this revelation," Dr. Bajwa told me. " He traveled throughout India, Tibet, and Arabia teaching, until he passed away at age seventy."

The nurse opened the door just enough to allow her head to peek through, signaling our time was up.

"One more question before I go," I asked him. He nodded in agreement.

"When did you realize that your purpose was to become a doctor? You seem so well suited for this. I can't imagine you being anything else."

A warm, glowing smile returned to his face.

"My *vocation* is being a doctor." he said. "My *purpose* is to know God."

We stood and embraced, and I then realized what I saw in his eyes when I first came out of my coma. Dr. Bajwa expresses God's love through his work.

I asked him if I could stay in touch, and he told me that, though he doesn't normally give out his personal email, he would make an exception for me. He told me to keep him posted on my progress.

My Christmas break at home ended all too quickly, but I left feeling loved, revived, and hopeful.

On January 4th 2017, back in my Chicago apartment, I recalled the conversation with Dr. Bajwa, and researched the basic beliefs of Sikhism. The colorful headdress Dr. Bajwa wears captured my imagination from the first day I met him, coming out of my coma. I discovered that a core teaching of the Sikh faith is that all people are created equal. Sikhs initiated into the faith wear a turban, signifying equal status among the faith's followers.

I found that Sikhs believe in one God, and they respect all humans of every religion. The holy book of Sikhs, *Guru Granth Sahib* is believed to have been written by divinely inspired saints, who came from various societies and religions. Sikh philosophy indicates that human beings are born innately good. They also believe everything is a part of God and God is a part of everything.

This awakened a childhood memory. When I was five years old, shortly after my father passed away, I was helping my mother in the kitchen as usual. She was a deeply devoted Catholic, and as such, there were statues of saints and other religious symbols throughout the house. On the windowsill sat a wooden crucifix with a porcelain Jesus hanging on it.

Looking up at the figurine, I asked her this one question: "What is God?"

My mother bent down, and held my face with both hands. "Oh, honey, God—is a little bit of everything," she told me.

Having seen similarities between these beliefs, compared to what I experienced in the Ethereal—I felt compelled to dig deeper. While researching Sikhism I came across another religion I had never studied before: Sufism, a sect of Islam with an emphasis on mysticism, inward worship, and the rejection of materialism. I wrote in my journal an aphorism that gave me a new perspective on the universal language of love:

Sane and insane, all are searching lovelorn for Him, in mosque, temple, church alike. For only God is the One God of Love, and Love calls from all these, each one His home.

—Sufism

When I became part of the web in the Ethereal, I understood that if I hurt myself, I hurt everyone around me, but whenever I loved, the light also spread. When I saw Maria there, her eyes were filled with the spiritual light that animates all life. She only said three words: *Just love me.* I had an awareness that love and light were entwined with one another. That was easy to see in spirit, but what does love look like in the temporal world, and how does it manifest?

I thought about what Pastor Man told me that day on my porch: "Give back to God by serving others in all your works. The divine nature will begin to express itself more fully through the gifts of the spirit—kindness, faith, goodness, forgiveness, respect, and love."

I wondered where the idea, "The power of a single act" came from, but now I began to understand it. Love is the link between the physical and spiritual worlds. The expression of love is seen through the power of a single act—by serving others.

In early February I decided to accept Pastor Man's invitation to attend the Chinese Bible Church of Oak Park. The church was only a few miles from my apartment, in the quiet suburb of Oak Park Village. The old two-story red-brick building sits on the corner of a four-way intersection and was originally built by a different congregation. I was curious to see what attracted the Chinese to a nondenominational Christian church.

> LOVE IS THE LINK BETWEEN THE PHYSICAL AND SPIRITUAL WORLDS. THE EXPRESSION OF LOVE IS SEEN THROUGH THE POWER OF A SINGLE ACT— BY SERVING OTHERS.

When I entered the small, intimate building, I found Paul ready and waiting to introduce me to the parishioners. I was amazed to see the diversity of people and languages. There were three separate worship services; one in Mandarin, one in Cantonese, and one in English. The pastor for the English service, Pastor Raj, is from India. That first Sunday morning at the English-language service, Paul sat beside me to make sure I was comfortable.

The service began with a small group of musicians playing and singing inspirational songs, and, as everyone stood up and sang in unison, the room filled with the same love, light, and connectedness I saw in the web. The more we sang, the more our hearts opened, and the more the light spread. After the service, all three congregations meet in the basement to enjoy a freshly prepared lunch of the most aromatic, delicious Chinese food I've ever tasted. This was a time of sharing stories, enjoying the food of different cultures, and rejoicing in the similarities of our own humanity.

I continued to attend each Sunday, and on March 5th Pastor Raj quoted a scripture during his sermon that brought deeper meaning to the idea of serving others.

For it is God who works in you, to will and act, in order to fulfill His good purpose.

–Philippians 2:13

Sitting in the pew, I thought about how Paul was an example of someone living the power of a single act. Until this all happened, I saw his personality as one of boundaries and professionalism—Paul is not a hugger. After my heart attack, Paul was my advocate at work who lobbied to keep me employed. Before I was released from the hospital he loaned me everything from dishes to lamps, helping my brothers set up my apartment. When he saw me struggling, he took a risk by inviting Pastor Man to visit me, thereby opening up his personal life while still remaining my work supervisor. Somehow he found the time to take me on regular walks at a nearby park, and to look after me when I came back into the office part time.

My brothers continued to come from Pittsburgh and Washington, DC on a regular basis, sacrificing time and money, away from their jobs and families to serve me any way they could. Occasionally their wives accompanied them, along with my nieces and nephew. Even when they couldn't make the trip, not a day went by without a phone call. They too have epitomized the power of a single act. To be the recipient of service is humbling in such a way that it has made me a more grateful and compassionate person.

After the service I went down into the basement for lunch, and some of the Chinese parishioners shared their conversion stories with me. An older woman who fled communist China in her late teens sat across the table from me. We had made some small talk in the weeks prior, and although I never knew her name, I felt comfortable enough to broach the subject. Shyly I asked her what made her convert to Christianity.

She looked back at me with an expressionless face, but her eyes telegraphed the answer. I could feel her pain as she paused, sensing that she was recalling memories of being subdued and oppressed. I was sorry I asked the question, and I wanted to tell her that it's okay not to answer, but she replied in broken English.

"In China, we are not free to worship openly. To me, God represents freedom."

"So, were you an atheist?" I asked her. "Did you believe in God before you converted?"

"I didn't know what God was," she explained, "but I knew there was something more inside me."

"Something more?" I asked, sensing her slight discomfort.

She glanced down at her plate of food, then replied, "You can't build a human being in a factory."

Freedom. Until then I never thought of God as freedom. When I was in the Ethereal, I never felt so free. Free of the pain in my body, free of regrets, free of doubt, free to love openly.

When I got back to my apartment that Sunday morning, I finished reading Eknath Easwaran's book, *Conquest of Mind*. It is a summary translation of the *Bhagavad Gita* (Hindu Scripture) and the *Dhammapada* (Buddhist Scripture). I came across a statement that to me is the crux of the book, and I immediately wrote it in my journal:

Only when choosing in freedom does the human being truly come to life.

—Eknath Easwaran

I pondered what the woman at lunch told me. The "something more" inside her was God's love and light, and you can't "build" that into a human being in a factory. I think about the Sikhs' belief, that human beings are born innately good. God gives us the freedom to choose love, and when we do, we come to life. Love exists because of free will.

> GOD GIVES US THE FREEDOM TO CHOOSE LOVE, AND WHEN WE DO, WE COME TO LIFE. LOVE EXISTS BECAUSE OF FREE WILL.

I think about the Pastor I met on the flight to Seattle, who spent the first half of his life in the darkness. When the darkness left him for dead, it was out of free will that he *asked* for help and God's free will *chose* to save him. The light shone down on him, literally, as he lay on the deck of his yacht baking in the sun. He let God in, spending the second half of his life, *fulfilling his good purpose.* This pastor then used his will to act out of service and love.

It also occured to me that only love, born through a magnanimous, loving creator, can forgive. I thought about the different paths each religion asks their followers to take, yet beneath them all, lies the same belief that *God is love.*

The more I researched how other religions also believe that God is love, the more my experience in the Ethereal felt validated. I had known from my Christian upbringing the two main tenets Jesus preached were synonymous: *Love God with all your heart, mind, and soul. Love your neighbor as yourself.* He also said that all the commandments are summed up in those words. The Apostle James went as far to call '*Love your neighbor as yourself*' God's "Royal Law."

While reading translations of the Bhagavad Gita, I found that in the Hindu tradition, the basic postulate of Saivism (those who revere the Lord Shiva) is *Love is the Supreme God.* This affirms the oneness of God and Love. I also discovered that the *Gita* was the doctrine that launched Mahatma Gandhi on his spiritual path. He was open to other world views and searched for universal principles that transcended religion as a dogma. To that end he wrote:

> *"If I would call myself, say, a Christian or a Mussalman, with my own interpretation of the Bible or the Koran, I should hesitate to call myself either. For then, Hindu, Christian, and Mussalman would be synonymous terms."*

One afternoon in early April I was walking through a city park near my apartment, enjoying the first signs of an early spring. I was thinking about how nature is the perfect expression of God's love. I stopped to rest on a park bench and at my feet was a bed of moss. Looking at the moss I was reminded of another time that nature was the conduit that God used to speak into Melanie's spirit, answering her prayers.

Maria was about seven years old and had been in a period of rapid decline. This was before we received a diagnosis of Rett Syndrome. She had been misdiagnosed several times before and we were faced with trying to solve the mystery on our own, based on her symptoms. Exhausted and hopeless, we drove to the mountains in Blowing Rock, North Carolina to rest. While walking through the lush green forest, Melanie was constantly in silent prayer, asking what to do next for Maria.

I was walking ahead of Melanie when I realized she no longer trailed me. As I turned back to look for her, I saw her bent over a pile of rocks on the hillside, covered in glowing green moss. Light beams pierced through the tall pine trees, reflecting light from the early morning mist into a kaleidoscope of colors. I stopped dead in my tracks, careful not to disturb the moment, because I knew something magical was unfolding. The forest had become her ally, brimming with life, helping to renew and reconnect her to the surrounding divine intelligence.

She caressed the moss, delighting in its texture and luminescent green glow. The moss shared its unique beauty, giving of itself freely and becoming a soothing balm for her wounds. The more she caressed, the more she relaxed into the moment, becoming playful and childlike, as if she were petting a puppy dog. Then, seemingly out of nowhere, she looked out into the forest and spoke the words given her: *Remove the obstacles.*

I walked up the trail and approached her.

"What do you mean, 'remove the obstacles'?"

She sprang up from the ground and rattled off her epiphany.

"We have to change her diet, it's inflaming her gut. Poison is in her food, poison is in our environment, toxic cleaning products, fragrances, indoor air quality, chemicals in the water—she's reacting to everything! Her senses are being over-stimulated. Too much TV, videos, chaos. We have to remove all these obstacles so her body has a chance to heal itself. Yes, that's it! And her meds—she's over medicated. I have to find a more natural way to deal with her symptoms. The answer is right in front of me. I can see it now!"

We finished our walk that morning and headed home to start anew. I took courses on how to create a non-toxic environment in our home and it transformed our living space. We also completely changed Maria's diet and her gut slowly began to heal. As I did my part on the physical aspects of our home, Melanie started down the path of integrative medicine. Her background as a pharmacist already prepared her with what she needed to put it into practice.

The cumulative effects on Maria were astounding, as many of her symptoms were mitigated and her quality of life improved. All these changes came as a direct answer to prayer, from the silent voice of a loving Creator, whispered through nature.

When I finished my walk and returned to my apartment, I picked up my research again and came across hints about what love looked like to the indigenous people of our country when the land was untouched by modernization. I found that the Apache expressed their central belief this way:

It makes no difference as to the name of God, since love is the real God of all the world.

The last week of April, I returned to the University of Chicago Medicine for my regular checkup. Dr. Uriel burst through the door in his characteristically energetic style.

"All your test results are perfect!" he told me. "Your new heart shows no signs of rejection or infection, so I've decided to let you go home earlier than expected. You can get your blood work done locally, but you still need to come back every three months for the other tests."

"Nir, I don't know what to say, I'm–"

"However," he interrupted, "I'm very concerned about your prostate cancer spreading. We will continue to monitor your PSA, and when the time comes, be prepared to stay here for a week to have the prostate removed... OK?"

Looking back at Nir, I saw an empathy in his eyes I had not recognized before. At that moment he was not practicing medicine—he was practicing love.

I got to my apartment that afternoon and before I started the process of getting organized to move home, I took some time to research Judaism. I want to know more about Dr. Uriel's Jewish heritage.

The core commandment of Judaism in the holy book of the Torah is *Love your neighbor as yourself.*

It is strange and wonderful how over the next two weeks I wrapped up my life in Chicago so quickly that it felt like watching a movie on rewind, putting everything back to the way it was before I arrived. I returned what Paul loaned me, donated my bed and miscellaneous belongings I accumulated over the past eleven months, and packed up the rest. Before I knew it, my brother Lou and his friend arrived with a truck to load up the furniture he loaned me, and I watched the city of Chicago get smaller and smaller in the rear-view mirror.

Now it was the third week of May and I was back home with my family. Almost immediately I returned to working full time. The joy of being alive and at home with Melanie and Maria was overwhelming. More than ever, I wanted to see doctors Patel and Carson, to not only express my gratitude, but also to learn more about how their individual beliefs played a role in their vocations. I was able to contact Dr. Patel and we decided on a time and place to meet.

On August 28th, 2017, I walked into the CaroMont Regional Medical Center cafeteria with a dozen roses wrapped in cellophane to meet Dr. Patel. Standing in the middle of the room trying to recall her face, I could feel my donor heart pounding with anticipation. I heard a voice behind me.

"Hey, Rob, I'm right here."

I turned and saw her glistening brown eyes, immediately transporting me back to the first time I saw her at my bedside, the second morning after coming out of a coma. The roses fell from my hands onto the table as I hugged her.

"Oh, Dr. Patel, I can't tell you how happy I am to see you!"

We'd had several conversations by phone, but this was the first time I saw her in person.

"Same here," she replied with a satisfied smile. "I've been keeping up with you through Lou. He sent me that video of you in the Rocky outfit… great stuff!"

After sharing a good laugh, we took a seat and I got right to the point.

"I know you don't have much time, and I've told you a good bit about my spiritual experience on the phone, but can we sit and chat for a moment? "

"Sure, I have a moment. Let's sit down."

"I'm curious about your religious beliefs," I told her. Dr. Patel didn't seem offended, signaling that it was OK to continue. "Are you Hindu?"

"Yes, I am Hindu," she responded without hesitation.

"Do you think God saved my life that night?"

"To some extent, yes. God gave me the knowledge, compassion, and patience to help me become a physician and to help save lives. God is the ultimate healer, protector, and Savior."

"Then why did you qualify your statement with 'to some extent'? Do you mean free will?"

"Yes, free will. I still had to take action to resuscitate you that night."

Free will. I think about how free will and love are intertwined. I felt her desire to serve others, and I felt love radiating from her. She chose every day to express that love through dedicated work.

Love becomes real in this world through our actions, since God both expresses and experiences life through us.

Early one morning, after Dr. Carson was done working the night shift, we met for coffee at a Dunkin' Donuts near the hospital.

I had not seen his face since the day I was discharged in early February 2016. I was sitting at a small table near the window, watching the parking lot for a "doctor type" to arrive. I saw a

LOVE BECOMES REAL IN THIS WORLD THROUGH OUR ACTIONS, SINCE GOD BOTH EXPRESSES AND EXPERIENCES LIFE THROUGH US.

pickup truck pull into the lot and a tall, lanky guy wearing scrubs get out. He spotted me through the window and pointed, smiling to indicate that he recognized me. I would not have picked out his face in a crowd since we'd only met once.

We shook hands and, after some pleasantries, I asked him why he did so much to save me that night.

"It didn't look like you were going to make it," he explained, "and we threw everything we had at you. You seemed to be reaching up in spirit, so I reached down and met you halfway. I tried to tip the scales and increase the odds in your favor. I had to give you every chance to survive. But in the end, I knew it was between you and your maker."

"Oh, then you believe in God?" I asked him.

"Yes," he said. "I am a Christian and my faith makes me a better doctor."

I asked him how, and he explained.

"I see God in the minutiae and details of things. If I had caught a red light that night and not made it into the hospital when I did, you probably wouldn't be here. I was in the right place at the right time, and I see that as God's time. I see God in the pauses between things, and in the empty spaces. There are no coincidences. You're meant to be here."

I thought about this conversation for weeks. When we serve others, love connects us to the higher realm. We can feel and sense our spirit lifting out of our clay vessel, defying gravity, and reaching for the heavens. The hand of God is waiting, ready to reach down and meet us halfway, but only when we choose to act. Our prayers hang in midair, powerless, unless action follows. Doing the deed demolishes the ego and gets us out of our own way so God can work through us.

> LOVE CANNOT EXIST WITHOUT FREE WILL. LOVE IS PROOF THAT GOD EXISTS.

Love cannot exist without free will. Love is proof that God exists.

170

GIFTS OF ADVERSITY

I was driving through El Paso, Texas in February of 2018 to see a client, and I heard a story on the radio so compelling that I pulled off the road into a parking lot and took out my notepad.

Early in the fifth century, a contemplative monk named Telemachus felt God call into his spirit to leave his monastic life, and so he made the trek to Rome not knowing why. As he approached the city, he heard the collective chanting and screaming of a large crowd coming from the Roman Colosseum.

Bewildered by what could attract so many people, Telemachus walked into the stadium and was horrified by the savagery and brutality before him. Gladiators were ripping each other's flesh apart with swords and spears while the drunken crowd cheered them on. Lions and tigers on the edge of starvation were kept in pits on the stadium floor and released to devour the vanquished.

Shocked by the extreme cruelty, Telemachus pushed his way onto the arena floor with the innocence of a child. He stood between two gladiators and shouted repeatedly, "In the name of God... stop!" The crowd was furious that someone would interfere with their entertainment, and began stoning him. Seeing the monk lying in a pool of blood covered with rocks, the stadium fell silent and heard his last words emanating from the pile of rubble: "In the name of God—somebody please stop this thing!"

Taken aback by the monk's death, one man in the upper tier of the stadium stood up and walked out. Emboldened by that act of courage, others followed in silence until the colosseum was almost empty. The Emperor Honorius was so moved by the event that he issued this decree:

> *"Rome no more should wallow in this old lust of Paganism and make her festal hour dark with the blood of man who murdered man."*

After the radio program finished, I got back on the road and contemplated the story's meaning. I could not have chosen a more poignant example to illustrate the power of a single act, which also tied into another concept I had been mulling over: the meaning of suffering.

Telemachus had no idea he would encounter such adversity or suffer a horrible death that day, yet the gift of his sacrifice ended one of the most shameful and barbaric periods of human history. His singular choice to listen to that inner voice, to enter the city and go into the stadium that day, ended the gladiator games and changed the history of the world.

I think about Maria and, through it all, the positive things that have come out of her life. Her suffering was the catalyst that drove me onto my knees that day to give her the coffee enema when she was sickened from toxemia. Had I chosen not to act in the face of adversity, Maria would have continued to needlessly suffer.

We can choose to accept things as they are or use our free will and take responsibility to change them. Melanie and I could have made vastly different choices, but as a result, Maria eats like a horse and has enough muscle tone to walk with assistance. Her spirit blesses our home every single day. It's a funny balance, though. I was a little too proactive and my ego thought I could fix everything by myself. It wasn't until God gave me *more* than I could handle that I learned dependence and trust. When I finally surrendered we experienced breakthroughs and answers that came from outside ourselves. That made all the difference.

What I learned is that adversity is an invitation to begin building a closer relationship with God. Had I not fallen to my knees that day to cleanse her, I would never have come face-to-face with the Divine. It was in doing the deed that God spoke into my spirit and said *Look at me, I'm right here.* The more we trust, the more we live in spirit and allow these gifts to manifest.

WHAT I LEARNED IS THAT ADVERSITY IS AN INVITATION TO BEGIN BUILDING A CLOSER RELATIONSHIP WITH GOD.

The meaning of life exists through the vicissitudes and struggles that draw us closer to God. I can hear Telemachus calling out in spirit through Maria's life: "In the name of God—somebody please stop this thing." That thing is called Rett Syndrome.

During our journey to help Maria, Melanie and I met a remarkable woman named Monica Coenraads. She also heard the call to "stop this thing," when her two-year-old daughter Chelsea was diagnosed with Rett Syndrome, and Monica sensed that "somebody" was her. As I got to know Monica, I was amazed at her background. I asked her why she was doing so much and she told me that it needed to be done.

"After the initial shock of Chelsea's diagnosis," she explained, "I stopped asking God 'why me' and said to myself 'why not me?' From that moment on I decided to do something about it. I wanted to know what Rett Syndrome was and to make sure everything was being done that needed to be. I refused to accept the status quo, and dug into the research. The more I researched, the more I realized much more needed to be done."

In 1999, Monica co-founded the Rett Syndrome Research Foundation to stimulate scientific interest, culminating with groundbreaking work in 2007. Scientists have now demonstrated in mouse models the first global reversal of the disorder's symptoms. She was awarded *Redbook* magazine's "Mother & Shaker Award," alongside Katie Couric and Matilda Raffa Cuomo. The Howard Hughes Medical Institute highlighted Monica's efforts in the 2006 November issue of the HHMI Bulletin.

Under Monica's leadership at RSRF and RSRT, over $79 million has been raised for Rett Syndrome research. The Rett Syndrome Research Trust has given more hope to children of Rett Syndrome and their families than any other institution in the world. Unimaginable gifts were born out of this mother's love when her spirit cried out, "In the name of God—somebody please stop this thing!"

I once asked Monica after all she's accomplished how the journey affected her personally.

"I've become a more positive and optimistic person," she told me, "because I have had to learn how to live in the *now*—solving the problem at hand and not focusing on the future."

I have come to believe that God is in the now, and the future is created by our free will. When "circumstances" like Rett Syndrome feel out of our control, how we handle that adversity creates the outcome.

When I returned home from the El Paso trip, my conversation with Monica remained in the back of my mind as I continued my daily routine, which was physically taxing after my heart transplant. The tasks of caring for a child with special needs are all-consuming. Melanie and I have a scant social life. Travel for rest and relaxation is rare, and we never fly together, should an accident occur leaving Maria without at least one of us to care for her. We relish the few precious moments that Melanie and I have together outside of work and caring for Maria. Paradoxically, I have become stronger through weakness—learning to depend more on God.

Focusing on the gifts Maria brought into our life and into the lives of others is a constant reminder of why we decided to have children. Like any parents, we hoped to see them do great things, to revel in their accomplishments, to be proud of the gifts they bring forth into the world to make it a better place for future generations. Maria fulfilled that dream in a different way than we ever could have expected. Many caregivers through the years found purpose and direction for their own lives working with Maria. Through her special life she taught me what it means to be human, by showing me that every human being has value. Maria holds a mirror in front of me, constantly reminding me that we are all a perfect expression of God's love. It's through children like Maria that we hear God whispering, *Look at me, I'm right here.*

Through the years, during our most trying days when Maria was in periods of rapid decline, Melanie and I would go for months living in and out of the hospital with little to no sleep. During those times when we were physically, emotionally, and financially on the verge of collapse, adversity pulled out all the stops, as if it was testing us.

Adversity would present itself through a doctor or hospital chaplain who would encourage us to institutionalize Maria. A stranger approached me once while in the hospital with Maria and said, "God wants you to be happy and get on with your life. Turn her over to the state before you and your wife lose everything. She'll be okay. God has a plan for her life."

"My wife and I brought her into the world," I replied, "and we are responsible for her care. *That's* God's plan for her life."

I learned that once I have done all that I can do, and it seems impossible to take another step, God's grace gives me the strength to continue. I think about the extraordinary gifts and life lessons I would have missed out on had I institutionalized Maria. She has been my spiritual teacher, in many ways confirming what I saw in the web, that we are all connected, and that one life is worth everything.

Ironically, people label those with disabilities as gimps, yet these special individuals most teach us what it means to be human, but free of ego, ulterior motives, judgement, and especially hate. In the quiet moments with Maria when she stares into my eyes, I hear the silent voice of God speaking through her saying *thank you, Maria for allowing me to show myself to the world*. God did not create her illness, but through her illness came the greatest gift of all—intimacy with the Creator.

In this same spirit, I think about all the gifts born through Chelsea Coenraad's life. New discoveries have been made in the field of gene therapy that can be applied to other potential cures. This is how the human race evolves. When life gives us adversity, God invites us to do something about it. Intellectual understanding is meaningless unless followed by action. We each have a choice: to let adversity draw out the best part of us and push us toward greatness, or to remain stuck.

> WE EACH HAVE A CHOICE: TO LET ADVERSITY DRAW OUT THE BEST PART OF US AND PUSH US TOWARD GREATNESS, OR TO REMAIN STUCK.

One Saturday morning in late March, as I was preparing Maria's breakfast I noticed an aphorism on the refrigerator door from an unknown author that I'd cut out of a magazine years ago. I forgot I'd taped it to the door with many other positive quotes to keep me inspired.

"No affliction would trouble a child of God if he knew God's reason for sending it."

Standing in front of the fridge door, I held Maria's breakfast in my hands and listened on the monitor for her to awaken. I thought about all the time in the past I wasted blaming God for not only Maria's sickness, but for adversity in my own life. Most of my real problems, however, were created by my choices that allowed fear and anger into my life, leading to the most destructive force of all—hatred. What I experienced was that hatred fed on itself, darkened my spirit, and led to self-destruction in silent, insidious ways. Hate destroys the clay vessel that carries it—but love rebuilds it.

In early April I was on the tarmac in Dallas waiting for my delayed flight to depart. The flight was oversold and seats had to be shuffled around at the last minute to accommodate all the passengers. A tall, well-dressed man got bumped out of first class and forced into the middle seat between me and another passenger.

WHAT I EXPERIENCED WAS THAT HATRED FED ON ITSELF, DARKENED MY SPIRIT, AND LED TO SELF-DESTRUCTION IN SILENT, INSIDIOUS WAYS. HATE DESTROYS THE CLAY VESSEL THAT CARRIES IT— BUT LOVE REBUILDS IT.

Once in flight, I pulled out my journal and began to write some thoughts. I was contemplating the nature of prayer, trying to come to terms with the most perplexing conundrum of all: why does God answer some prayers but not others? I noticed the man beside me glancing at my notebook, so I subtly reached for a magazine and laid it on top.

"Sorry, I didn't mean to impose," he said, "but seeing what you're writing about... well, I'm curious what you do for a living?"

"I'm a sales rep for a steel company. How about you?"

"I work for myself," he said. "Financial advisor–" He stopped midway through his sentence and shook his head. He looked confused. "But back to you... what's a sales rep doing writing about prayer?"

"Well, I had a near death experience about two years ago," I told him, "and I'm still trying to make sense of it. Writing about it is cathartic, and seeing it on paper helps me understand what happened."

He twisted his body around in the seat to face me the best he could in those tight quarters.

"What did you see? Did you see the light?"

"Actually, I saw many lights," I told him, "and each one represented a life—it was an interactive web that binds us all together. Everything is connected, both animate and inanimate objects—we are all one. I even saw my daughter who is severely handicapped and has never spoken my name. But in that place, she was perfect and whole."

He stared at me with widened eyes. It felt like we were standing still, but the plane was going 500 mph. Everything around me faded out as if we were the only two people floating through the air. The deafening white noise inside the plane made the moment even more surreal, until he broke the silence.

"Okay... you have to meet this guy who works with me here in Dallas. I want him to know, after everything he's going through right now, what awaits him on the other side. I also think he can help you answer some questions about prayer."

I asked him who the guy was and what happened to him, and he explained that he's a successful businessman named John Paine, who was diagnosed seventeen years ago with ALS (Lou Gehrig's disease) while he was in his mid-forties.

"This guy had it all," he told me. "Wealth, prestige, beautiful family, you name it. Now he's in a wheelchair paralyzed from head to toe, dependent on a ventilator for his next breath, and in excruciating pain every minute. Yet... he still comes into the office every single day."

"What? You've got to be kidding me!"

"Not only that," he told me. "A short documentary film was just made about John's journey and what he's learned along the way. It's called *The Luckiest Man*. He's also working on a book so he can share his story. That's why you two guys need to meet, and I'm going to arrange it."

"*The Luckiest Man?*" I asked him. "Interesting title given how much this guy has suffered all these years. Why do you think he can help me understand the nature of prayer and how it works?"

"Because all John wants to do now is share how his battle with ALS led him into an intimate relationship with God, and what he calls 'real living.' He also talks a lot about how his prayers for physical healing were never answered and how he came to terms with that."

When I heard those words, *his prayers for physical healing were never answered,* my donor heart beat rapidly and my mouth went dry as I thought about my upcoming prostate biopsy to determine how much farther the cancer had spread. I wondered how my prayer for healing would be answered, and was reminded of the day I heard Pastor Eric's sermon on my spiritual encounter with Frosty. After that portion of the sermon, he discussed a woman in the parish who was battling an aggressive form of cancer. She was a beloved member of the congregation and community.

Pastor Eric commented that he had never seen so many people pray for her healing. The longer the battle raged on, the toll it took on her and her family became untenable. Her treatments left her in unbearable pain, and her children became deeply affected watching their mother suffer endlessly; their school grades plummeted. Insurance wouldn't cover all the bills and the family was on the verge of bankruptcy.

In that circumstance, it felt like God did answer everyone's prayers, but not in the way we all hoped. He granted her the ultimate healing by taking her into the kingdom of love and light. Having come back from that place, I can attest that she was home and she was whole.

I realized that I was still not ready to let go. I wanted God to answer my prayer the way I thought it should be answered, because the idea of cancer taking me down now was terrifying. The same fears and doubts I had when I first came out of my coma came sneaking back into my awareness. *Who will look after my family? Will Melanie have enough money to care for Maria? Can she do it on her own?*

The man next to me on the plane agreed to set up a meeting for me to meet John Paine the first week in May. The day rolled around quickly and I found myself in Dallas, in a prestigious commercial high-rise building, walking down a long hallway that led to his office. I opened the door and a soft-spoken young man, John's assistant Leo, greeted me. He told me John was expecting me, as he led me through the foyer toward a corner office with the door cracked halfway open. My palms were sweaty and my breath short in anticipation of meeting this man. I had no idea what to expect, and I felt like I was intruding on the little time he might have left. I wondered if maybe I shouldn't have brought my notepad and tape recorder. Hopefully they wouldn't offend him.

As Leo nudged the door wide open, I saw John sitting in his high-tech wheelchair next to a large round table made with elegant ceramic tile. The two bay windows behind him flooded the room with dazzling sunlight, blocking out everything else in my periphery.

John was dressed in slacks and a button-down shirt. His paralyzed hands were in his lap, covered with a small brown blanket.

He looked like the quintessential executive, handsome with short, meticulously combed gray hair. A tube ran up the back of his wheelchair from an oxygen tank mounted beneath it. A strap wrapped around his head kept a breathing device secured in his nostrils, forcing air into his lungs.

"Rob!" John shouted with enthusiasm mixed with the struggle to breathe. He gulped for air and invited me in. "Sit next to me."

Leo offered a warm look as I approached his boss.

"I'll be right outside your door, Mr. Paine, if you need anything."

My body released some tension and I quickly connected with John as I pulled up a chair to sit beside him. In that moment these words came to my mind: *Adversity is the great equalizer. There is no escaping the human condition.*

"I can't thank you enough for taking the time to see me," I told him. "I just want you to know–"

"Are you kidding?" he interrupted me with a wide smile. "I've been looking forward to this. First, just one favor... If my head falls forward, don't panic. Just lift it gently back onto my headrest cradle, okay?"

"Yes, of course," I assured him. Caring for Maria got me well accustomed to such supportive responses. He thanked me and we continued.

"Before we get started, let's pray that God blesses this meeting," he said. "Go ahead and put your hand on my leg so we can touch and agree."

John closed his eyes and prayed that our time was well spent, and that we learned from each other. He then asked me to tell him about my experience. He tires easily and I only had an hour to spend with him, so I gave him a short summary of what I experienced in the Ethereal and then asked him some questions.

"One reason I wanted to meet with you is that after coming back into the world, I struggle with how to remain dependent on God while working full time."

John took in a gulp of air through the breathing device. He could only manage a few words at a time before filling his lungs back up.

"Yes, that is at the heart of what I have learned. Dependence on God has been the greatest gift. I wouldn't change my situation, because ALS gave me a relationship with God."

I asked him how the relationship developed.

"I learned that I was the one who had to let God into my life. Once I did, I began to see that the greatest treasures on Earth are relationships, first with God and then with others. I saw how my thinking had gone awry. You know those crazy thoughts that all my relationships would be great if it weren't for the *other people*."

We shared a laugh and he continued.

"God showed me that I was the common denominator in judging others. He helped me remove blockages in myself so I could have richer relationships. When I allowed Him to be the God of me, I was finally able to receive love."

In between sentences he paused to catch his breath.

"I don't think we naturally come wired with unconditional love. You know when we were growing up and did the right things, we got praise from our parents and we translated that as love. We interpreted love as conditional."

"I experienced that unconditional love in the Ethereal and it changed everything," I told him.

"When I became filled with love, then I was finally able to truly love others," he said. "That's what I call *real living.*"

I asked him what he'd learned about success and he shared his experience.

"Here's what they don't tell you," he said. "Success cannot bring healing to your hidden wounds. It cannot validate you, and it never quenches your thirst for more. It puts words in your mouth—*I'll show them* or *look at me.* In the end, none of the success brought me what I hoped it would. Instead it left me wanting more. I sacrificed relationships with the people dearest to me and was oblivious to it. God's grace stopped me from sabotaging my life through wanting to always be in control. God's grace has a way of shaking us free—if we're willing to be shaken—and sometimes he uses the people we least expect to do so."

At that moment I realized that Maria had been that person for me. I thought about what I might have become, how hollow my life would have been without her. She shook me to my foundation, drove me to my knees, and challenged me to be more. It was in my weakness that she introduced me to God. She is the one who showed me what "real living" means.

I asked John the question that was in my journal the day I met his colleague on the plane. Namely, about his current thoughts on prayer.

"Your prayers of healing were never answered the way you thought during these years, right?" I asked him.

"My greatest fear when I was first diagnosed was that I would just exist and not be able to contribute," he explained. "But that was then. Fifteen years have passed and today I am paralyzed from head to toe, relying on machines for every breath and totally dependent upon others. Yet, my life today is far from mere existence. See, the presence of God is what produces abundant living. What I enjoy now is far greater than anything ALS could take away. My life's purpose and joy is to help others get closer to God, and to walk with Him. That's real living!"

I could see that John was close to being exhausted, so I asked him just one final question.

"The world is afraid of suffering. But how do you see it?"

"This rhythm of suffering has worked its miracle in my life," he said, "giving me intimacy with God and oneness with His presence. Suffering allowed me to dismiss the God of anger, perfection, and judgement, and embrace the God of unconditional love. I want to tell everyone to rest in that love, even in the pain. Allow that love to wash over you, to validate you. Become more vulnerable to that love... just trust it."

He paused to regain enough strength for one final thought.

"I've been asked what I'd give to be rid of this disease. What if I could hold my wife one more time, if I could bounce my grandchildren on my lap or hug my children, if I could put in a full day at the office, if I could lead thousands into professions of faith—if I could do it all but had to trade this intimacy with God born from ALS. Would I do it? The choice is easy... I would keep this disease. I'd take this pain, this slow suffocation. I wouldn't trade this intimacy for anything. This torture has been used for my salvation, and I'm thankful for it every day."

On the plane ride home I sketched in my journal and realized John gave me a clue to the vexing question of the interplay between circumstances, God's will, and the will of a human

185

being. It ties into what Dr. Carson told me when we met at Dunkin' Donuts.

"It didn't look like you were going to make it and we threw everything we had at you," he said. "You seemed to be reaching up in spirit, so I reached down and met you halfway. I tried to tip the scales and increase the odds in your favor. I had to give you every chance to survive. But in the end, I knew it was between you and your maker."

God calls to the best part of us through circumstances, and with our free will we can choose whether or not to answer.

When adversity comes—and it eventually comes to all of us—it's God's way of telling us something, asking us to do something, or asking us to let go of something. Adversity introduces us to our authentic selves and reminds us who we are.

ADVERSITY INTRODUCES US TO OUR AUTHENTIC SELVES AND REMINDS US WHO WE ARE.

The second week of May I found myself lying on a table in the fetal position with my bottom exposed in the Urology Department at the University of Chicago Medical Center. The same two female assistants that prepared me for my prostate biopsy in April 2016 began the process of sterilizing the area of treatment and lining up the surgical tools on a stainless steel table. As each tool hit the table with a *clink*, the muscles in my stomach tightened, anticipating the pain.

My urologist entered the room and told me what to expect. Instead of the standard six-core sample biopsy, this time he'd be taking an aggressive fifteen-core sample to determine just how far the cancer has spread. He told me that results take about two weeks, and then we'd schedule surgery.

I couldn't find a comfortable sitting position on my flight back to Charlotte the next morning. The discomfort from the biopsy radiated from the inside out. To take my mind off the procedure, I thought about my conversation with John Paine when he said "This torture has been used for my salvation." That sentiment brought me peace in the moment.

May 31st, 2018 I received a phone call from my urologist's assistant.

"Mr. Gentile," he said, "I uh, well, I'm not sure how to explain this, but the biopsy results indicate that you're cancer free. There was no trace of it in any of the samples." There was a silence between us as he awaited my reaction.

I think about the day Dr. Uriel came into my room, told me I had prostate cancer, and took me off the transplant list. I thought it was the end of the road—I thought I was finished. Now I think that God used my circumstance to answer the prayers of many with prostate cancer who are now being transplanted because of my case.

Had I not made an impassioned plea to Dr. Uriel to find a way to transplant me, and had he not used his free will to rally his team, a new category for transplantation would never have been created. Medical history would not have been made.

It also confirmed what I saw in the web, that we are all connected in ways far beyond my understanding. I thought about the scripture verse I had read in the hospital during that time.

"For as the heavens are higher than the earth, so are my ways higher than your ways and my thoughts than your thoughts."

—Isaiah 55:9

"Hello... Mr. Gentile? Are you still there?"

"I'm sorry," I told him. "I just... let me ask you a question. How does cancer just go away? Especially having been on immune suppressants for almost two years now. I thought the reverse would be true, and that it should have spread?"

"All I can say is that it was very small".

"Are you saying I never had cancer?"

"No, you had cancer," he told me, "we were sure of it. There was a lot at stake to take you off the transplant list. Then Dr. Uriel put his reputation on the line for you. I'm looking at your original biopsy right now and there is no question about it, you had cancer. But now we're just as sure that this biopsy is showing no signs of cancer."

I was bewildered but grateful with my entire being. Now that I was cancer free I decided to pursue learning more about my donor heart. I already wrote one letter to Gift of Hope (the organ donation agency) on my first-year anniversary, with no response from the donor family. I held off from reaching out again because they'd already experienced one loss with the death of their loved one. With the imminent threat of cancer, I didn't want to put them on another emotional roller coaster. What if I died from cancer and they felt that the heart had been a wasted gift? With that behind me now, it was important to find out who was living inside me. Something kept tugging at me. Night and day I had feelings that were not my own and that wouldn't let me rest. So I dropped a second letter in the mailbox.

SPIRITUAL BEINGS,
CLAY VESSELS

My donor heart pounds so hard it's all I can hear as I hold a letter in my hands from the University of Chicago Medicine. Standing on my front porch I left the rest of the mail in the box and tore open the envelope. The letter inside was printed on thick, official-looking cardstock. *Finally I get to know who is living inside me.* I pulled out the letter with joyful anticipation.

> **You are invited to attend a special event, Courage and Innovation: Celebrating Heart Transplantation on Saturday, February 23, 2019 at the University of Chicago.**

The disappointing feeling was no longer singular. It was magnified and shared by the heart beating inside me. I felt for the first time that this person inside me had been waiting to be heard. We were both on this mission together; we both had something to learn from the other. Whatever it took, I had to find out who it was. I booked two plane tickets for Melanie and me to attend the event. Maybe I could make a personal connection with Gift of Hope or find someone else who could help me identify the donor family.

The event, held in the Rubloff Auditorium at the Art Institute of Chicago, began with the fifty-year history of heart transplantation and the medical milestones that made it possible. Doctors Uriel and Jeevanandam co-directed the formal event, followed by dinner and a gala celebration.

I was standing in line at the buffet table and saw a woman who was transplanted a few months before me. We met back in early 2017 during a heart transplant support group meeting, and I remember her telling the group she had contacted her donor family. I approached and reminded her where we met. She remembered me as "the guy from North Carolina who got a heart."

"Yep, that's me."

"Weren't you also a clinical trial patient for the NuPulse?"

"Wow, great memory!"

She offered a warm smile and I rushed to the point.

"Look, Kay, from one alien to another–"

She burst out laughing and I continued...

"I need some advice. I've written two letters to Gift of Hope, but haven't heard anything. I realize the donor's family has the right not to respond, but something tells me the donor wants to be heard. I know that sounds crazy but–"

"I'll tell you what crazy is," she broke in. "After transplant, all I craved was chocolate milk, and I have never been a fan. It got to the point that I drank all the chocolate milk on the eighth floor and the nurses had to get milk from the other floors to satisfy me. They thought I was insane—until I met with the donor mother. Turns out my donor was addicted to chocolate milk!"

"Uncanny!" I agreed. I practically begged her to tell me how she found out, and she explained that I needed to call "this wonderful woman named Susan" at Gift of Hope here in Chicago.

"Tell her we talked, and I promise she'll help you the best she can."

The last week of February I called Susan and gave her some medical details. She opened my file and explained that the donor's father called the agency after receiving my second letter last year and wanted to know more about me.

"We told him that release forms had to be signed by both parties," she said, "but we never heard back from him. That's why we didn't contact you."

I asked her to email me the form so I could sign it on the spot.

"Can you call him? Tell him I'll come to him, meet him anywhere. I just want to know more about his son... can't you tell me anything!?"

There was a long silence between us, and I realized I pushed her too far.

"I can't tell you anything until the father gives me permission," Susan told me. "Gift of Hope is protective of donor families, and we treat them with the utmost respect. If a donor family wants to meet with you, they consider it a sacred opportunity for both families, but it is always up to them. Depending on the nature of the death, some recipients never get to know the identity of the donor. For some families it's just too emotional."

I let out a deep breath and told her I understood. She took a compassionate tone with me.

"I'm reading the letters you wrote," she said, "because we screen them and keep them on file before releasing them to the donor family. I see you have a special needs child and you mention in the letter how this gift of life you received also saved Maria, because you were able to get back to work and provide for your family. That's what we're all about here—the celebration of life, so–"

"Yes?!" I interrupted her, anticipating good news.

"So, I see the father's phone number in the file and I'm going to reach out to him on your behalf. After all, he did contact us. So that tells me he's open to the idea of meeting you."

"Oh, Susan that would be incredible!" I told her "I can't begin to thank you for your help!"

"Well, let's see where this goes," she said.

She emailed the release form and told me she'd contact me after she spoke with the father.

On March 20th she called back with good news. She got the release. The father agreed to meet with me... I was elated.

"I can't believe it," I shouted. "Tell me, tell me everything, how did he die, who is he—I mean what's his son's name?"

"Daughter," she broke in. The phone went silent.

"Daughter... what do you mean *daughter*?"

"Her name is Molli," Susan told me. "She was twenty years old."

"*She?* A girl? Twenty years old... that means she was born at the same time– Okay this is freaking me out," I told her. "She's Maria's age... born in 1996—only twenty? What happened?!"

"I'm sorry, Rob. That's all I can tell you. It's up to the father, Jay, whether he wants to share the details. I'll email you his cell number. He told me you can call him directly to set up a meeting place."

About a month after that call with Susan, I found myself in a Denny's restaurant an hour north of Chicago. Jay sent me a text: *Running ten minutes late, need more time to gather the photos you asked for and charge her laptop.*

I was relieved. I needed more time to process this fusion of thoughts and feelings taking place inside me. I couldn't discern if these feelings were coming from me or Molli. They rushed in and I tried to feel each one individually, but it was no use. They came at me too quickly. They were foreboding feelings like loneliness, regret, and sadness. But also joy, relief, and love. I wondered which ones were hers and which ones were mine?

How can I feel lonely after experiencing the web? Are these Molli's feelings?

The collective clanking sound of silverware on plates and multiple conversations became a background blur. I was snapped out of it as the door opened and I spotted a tall, lanky man wearing a ball cap and looking around. He carried a large silver laptop and a manila folder under his right arm. I took several steps toward him and extended my hand.

"Jay?"

"I guess that means you're Rob," he said, straight-faced, returning the handshake.

"Molli's heart is really pumping hard right now, man!" I told him. "She must be happy to see you. I need to sit down."

"Oh yeah?!" He finally smiled and we took a seat at a small, intimate booth. Jay laid the laptop on the table to his right, and the manila folder in the center. He had the cracked, calloused hands of a hard-working laborer. Both of us fidgeted with silverware, wrapped tightly in paper napkins, and moved them around as if we were playing a board game. Neither of us knew where to start, so I broke the ice.

"I can't thank you enough for meeting with me," I told him. "I just… well, I just want to know more about her. I want to honor her life and thank you and your–"

"So, what do you do for a living?" he broke in with a straight-forward tone.

I sensed he was not yet ready to talk about Molli, so I replied to his small talk and told him I was a sales rep for a steel company.

"I guess it came naturally for me because I'm from a steel town outside of Pittsburgh and worked in the mill when I got out of high school," I explained. Jay's face softened.

"Oh, that's cool," he said. "I work with steel all day at my job. We make freezers for restaurants and I operate the press that bends and shapes the steel sheets."

"What a coincidence, huh? And both our girls were born in 1996." Jay placed his hands on the table shoulder-width apart and nodded his head upward.

"Was Molli your only child?"

"Yeah."

He glanced down at the folder then back up at me.

"Girls have a special relationship with their daddies, don't they?" I said with a knowing smile.

Jay's chin quivered slightly as he pushed the folder toward me. Without hesitation I opened it and the first photograph I saw was a close up of Molli, a natural blonde with smooth, fair skin and large, sky blue eyes. She had an easy, natural smile revealing a slight gap between her two front teeth, giving her the unique look of a fashion model.

"She's so beautiful, Jay," I said, mesmerized by Molli's impossibly blue eyes that dominated every photograph. As I looked through the pictures, she was holding a different animal in almost every shot—but one in particular stood out. She's sitting next to a white, furry creature with large, expressive eyes like her own. It looks like a cross between a miniature camel and a sheep with a perpetual smile on its face. Molli was wearing a black tank top with her left arm extended toward the animal. I noticed some markings on her bicep and the inside of her forearm, but decided not to ask Jay about them.

"Easy to see she was an animal lover, huh?" I said with a chuckle. "What's this cute looking creature she's with in this photo?"

"That's an Alpaca, her favorite. Animals were everything to her."

"What else did she like?" Jay lowered his head, hiding his eyes behind the brim of his ball cap. "I'm sorry, I don't mean to ask a ton of questions. I just want to–"

"No, it's okay, man," Jay said, glancing over at the computer. "I don't use a computer at work and I'm not a letter writing kind of guy. That's why I called the agency after I got your second letter. I wanted to tell you what happened at Molli's celebration of life we have at the park next to her grave site."

I folded my hands in front of me and leaned back in the booth.

"I wasn't ready to read your second letter... I just couldn't. So I gave it to Molli's best friend, Natalie, to read before the balloon release. We all gathered around Natalie and everyone was in tears hearing about your daughter, how grateful you were for this gift of life and the other coincidences."

"Other coincidences?" I asked him.

"Molli was always drawn to special needs kids," he explained. "I mean, she would go out of her way to love on 'em no matter where she was. Like, if she saw a kid in a wheelchair at the mall passing by, she would yell out, 'God loves you! God bless you!' And she always stood up to bullies if they made fun of those kids. Molli was all heart. You know, from the time she was a child and learned how to spell her name, she always dotted the 'i' in Molli with a heart. It's engraved on her headstone that way too. That's why after reading your letter Natalie said 'I hope we get to meet this guy someday, because Molli would have picked him to get her heart.'"

Jay slid the computer in front of me.

"There's more photos and some of her artwork in here. She loved to draw, especially black and white pencil sketches."

I placed my hands on the laptop.

"Everybody loved Molli," he added. "She told me she had over 3,000 friends on Facebook. I don't know how to use this, but maybe you do. Go ahead and open it."

"Before I do that, I mean, if you're not comfortable telling me how she…"

"She committed suicide," he told me. My eyes were fixed open. I felt them burning, but I couldn't blink. Jay handed me a small artist's rendition photo of Molli that was given out during the balloon release. It's teal and purple with a ribbon in the bottom left hand corner indicating suicide prevention awareness. Before I could speak, he also handed me a pink and blue wristband that said "*Fly High Molli 1996 - 2016.*" I slid it on my wrist.

"What happened?" I asked him.

"I don't know... kids grow up differently than you and I did, with all this social media and stuff. When she was about fifteen, she started that cutting thing. That's when the darkness came. I took her to counseling once, but I don't think it helped."

"Cutting?" I thought about Molli's photo with the alpaca and the markings I noticed, but had no idea what that meant.

"I guess it's some of the crazy things kids do nowadays," he told me. "They cut their own skin. They think it's cool or something—I don't understand it."

Neither do I. I'd never heard of it. I guess I'm a little naïve as to how kids grow up these days. I tell him that my daughter, Maria, lives in a protective bubble.

"My wife and I hear about the constant pressure kids are under from peers and society," I said. "It's so hard for kids to fit in and feel accepted. I don't know about you, but growing up was hard enough for me without all this technology."

"No kidding," he agreed. "We didn't even know what a cell phone was, let alone a tweet. I thought that was something a bird does." We shared a laugh.

"You haven't mentioned her mom," I said. I couldn't read his face as he responded.

"We've been divorced a long time. I don't see her or talk to her. Molli was about eight or nine when her mother was diagnosed with cancer. That really changed her." He took a pause, but kept eye contact. "She got hooked on drugs and started hanging around with the wrong crowd. Molli would stay with each of us for a while, and then her grandmother, until she got a job and her own apartment."

I nodded my head sympathetically and opened the laptop. I reached for the power button, but I stopped cold as Jay slid a photo in front of me. It was Molli lying in her coffin at the funeral home.

Now he was ready to talk.

"When the cops came to get me at work that day to identify her I had to drive her car back to my place. She was listening to this crazy CD from some heavy metal band, and the song was about how cool suicide is—can you believe that?"

I was caught off guard. My right hand hovered over the power button, wanting to turn it on so I could escape the moment. The tragedy of losing such a beautiful human being this way was overwhelming. Molli's heart felt subdued. It was no longer pumping hard like it was a few minutes ago. The "we" in the me didn't want to see her like this.

Jay picked up the photo and pointed to the end of the coffin.

"See these shoes? I had to bring them to the funeral home so they could prop them up in there. I didn't know Molli was an organ donor, but in the end she gave away everything, man. Who knows how many lives she saved? She was all heart... and you got a great one."

I couldn't find words to speak in the moment, so I just stared back at Jay. My finger found its way to the power button and the computer screen lit up. I turned the laptop sideways so we could both see it. The first thing I noticed was a DVD playing in the background. The last movie Molli watched was *Alien*. Those foreboding feelings of loneliness and sadness that I felt earlier came washing over me again.

Is this how you felt, Molli, like an alien—alone and misunder-stood? What were you searching for?

I remember the two months after transplant, the first time I went to a heart transplant support group meeting at the hospital. Many patients suffered from depression and loss of identity having their birth hearts removed. One guy in the group cracked a joke, trying to lift everyone's spirits.

"Look at it this way," he said, "we'll always be special—we're aliens now."

I opened various folders on Molli's computer and found more photos. Now that I was aware of it my eye was drawn to the cuts, and they were on more than just her left arm. The photos revealed more cuts as she approaches age twenty, and the nat-ural, easy smile of her youth transformed into a masterful fake smile, hiding a pain that she would take to her grave.

I thought about what Jay said: "That's when the darkness came."

I was thinking about and feeling darkness in that very moment. *Is this why you want to be heard, Molli? Is this the tugging inside me that would not let me rest until I found you? What are you trying to tell me about the darkness and the light?*

These feelings are like the dark parts of the web I saw in the Ethereal. I wondered what the dark parts of the web rep-resented. Some parts are brighter than others, while some are almost completely black.

While in the web I thought, *If I hurt myself, I hurt everything connected to me. But if I love, the light will spread.* The web I saw looked like it was made of trillions of neurons, and each neuron had a quark of light inside that represented a life. The web was woven together like a tapestry of twinkling lights that stretched into infinity and hung on the ceiling of the universe, binding us all together.

Could Molli be showing me through her life experience what led her into the darkness?

Jay pointed to a folder on the computer screen, drawing me out of my own head.

"Click on this one," he told me. "I think some of her artwork is in there."

The first black and white drawing I saw was of a male and female bird perched together on a flower-laden branch. I was struck by the attention to detail and professional quality of the drawing. There was something else that seemed familiar about the style of her drawing, but it evaded me in the moment. I asked Jay if she took drawing lessons, but he told me it just came natural to her.

The second drawing was a bouquet of flowers consisting of three daisies. I'd seen this drawing before but couldn't place it. I closed the file and went back to some recent photos of Molli taken before that dreadful day. There it was—tattooed on her right shoulder—three large daisies with the stems extending down to her elbow.

Then I remembered a photograph of my father kneeling behind a row of daisies in front of his garden back home. That photograph had been passed down in our family for decades, and preserved the memory of him more than any other picture. The daisy was his favorite flower too. I took a deep breath, letting it out slowly while closing the laptop. I looked up at Jay.

"The coincidences keep piling up."

He raised his eyebrows and asked me how.

"My father's favorite flower was the daisy," I told him. Jay shook his head. "And my mother was also a natural born artist who loved to draw pencil sketches. She and Molli have strangely similar styles. The way they use lines and shading to express emotions... and their subjects are also alike."

Jay leaned in across the table.

"I wasn't sure before we met today," he said, "but... well... I'd like to invite you to Molli's next celebration of life coming up in June. It would mean a lot, especially to Natalie and Molli's other friends. Natalie arranges everything, so I'll give you her cell number. Do me a favor, though, let me tell her first you're going to call, because she's still really emotional. They've been best friends since they were five years old."

"I'm honored!" I told him. "And no worries, I'll wait a few days before calling Natalie."

The waiter approached our table for the third time.

"Have you guys decided on something?"

"No," he told her. "I'm gonna be late for work, so just water today." Jay stood up and laid a generous tip on the table. "Come on, I got something for you in my truck."

I followed Jay out to his truck and he handed me a T-shirt.

"Sorry... we gave out so many at her first balloon release that I only have extra-large left over. I think Molli's entire high school graduating class must have been there, so we didn't have them made again the second year."

The front of the shirt was a close up of Molli with the white Alpaca's nose pressed against her cheek. The back of the shirt read: *Your wings were ready but my heart was not.*

We shook hands and I slowly stepped backward away from the truck. Molli's heart was racing so fast I felt lightheaded and nauseated. My hands trembled, my body sweat, and it felt like I had to upchuck. *If I can just make it to my rental car and lock myself inside, we'll be okay.*

"Hey, you're gonna come, right?" Jay asked.

I was only three car lengths away from Jay, so I hollered back.

"Of course. You can count on it!"

Sitting inside my rental car, I resisted the temptation to dry heave by practicing the same deep breathing exercises I used when I awoke from transplant and Molli's heart pounded so hard it felt like I was being pushed out of bed. Now I understood that pounding was a harbinger of things to come. As my body relaxed I talked aloud with Molli.

"You know, kid, we're in this together now. I thought my journey would end when I found you, that I would finally have closure... but no. Did you push me to find you because you want to be heard? So, start talking! Sorry, it's okay, we'll figure it out together. You know what I've learned, Molli? Coincidences are God's way of remaining anonymous."

The next thing I knew I was on the airplane headed home, and I was so physically and emotionally exhausted that I fell into a deep but turbulent sleep. I entered a dream that illustrated my emotional state.

I was standing at the edge of a dark, gloomy forest. There was an eerie stillness in the woods. It was twilight, making it hard to see beyond the tree line. A light drizzle kept the fog close to the ground. I tried stepping forward to explore the woods, but I couldn't move. I saw something emerge from behind a tree and it was walking straight at me.

I realize it was a young girl with both arms extended in front, palms up. She came to a hard stop when her hands touched my chest, like a robot sensing something in front of it.

Her long hair was stringy and wet from the rain, and heavy mascara ran down her cheeks. She stared at me with lifeless eyes. I looked down at her arms and saw a series of cuts in perfect horizontal patterns from her wrist to her bicep.

"What are you trying to tell me?" I asked her. "Please talk to me."

She lowered her arms and stepped aside, as if she wanted to show me something. More girls emerged from behind the trees. As they walked toward me, they raised their pant legs and sleeves, revealing hidden cuts on their bodies. They had me surrounded, and were pushing in on me, but nobody was talking. I noticed their eyes all looked the same—dull, lightless, and without affect.

I frantically rotated around inside the tight circle and pleaded.

"I can't help you if you don't tell me why you're doing this. Somebody, please, talk to me!"

I heard a loud voice that woke me from my dream: "Flight attendants please prepare for landing."

Back home, Melanie anxiously waited to hear about my meeting with Jay. I sensed before I left that she harbored some misgivings about the trip, but I couldn't put my finger on it. After I finished sharing the details, she breathed an audible sigh of relief and opened up.

"When you discovered it was a woman's heart I freaked out," she said, "but I didn't want to tell you. It's just a biological fact that female hearts are smaller, and I assumed you wouldn't have the same longevity." Melanie paused and glanced down at the shirt Jay gave me. "But now I can see her heart was meant for you, both physically and spiritually."

"I think we both made assumptions," I told her. "When Jay told me about Molli's life I kept thinking about what Dr. O told me after the transplant. Do you remember what he said?"

203

"How can I ever forget?" Melanie replied, holding back tears. "He said, 'We put a Jaguar heart in you, kid.'"

"Yeah, that's right. We both *assumed* it was an athletic male."

"What are you thinking?" Melanie asked.

I hesitated for a moment.

"This might sound crazy, Melanie, but it feels like Molli speaks to me through my emotions, and lately through my dreams as well. It's like I can feel her trying to tell me something. Is there something she wants her family and friends to know?"

"How in the world are you going to find out?" Melanie wondered.

"Jay told me to call her best friend, Natalie. She knew Molli better than anyone. Before I do though, I want to follow up on something Dr. O told me...

"He said the heart contains its own system of neurons that rival the brain. The heart's neural networks interact with the brain, 'imprinting' and storing many of our personality traits and preferences. He also said that only time would tell if some of the donor traits will express themselves in me. It feels like Molli is expressing herself in a big way, so I'm going to research this before I call Natalie."

As I searched for answers I came across fascinating research conducted by the Heart Math Institute. They say the heart communicates with the brain in four ways: neurologically, biochemically, biophysically, (pulse waves), and energetically using electromagnetic fields. The heart is the most powerful source of electromagnetic energy in the human body, producing the largest rhythmic electromagnetic field of any of the body's organs. The heart's electrical field is about sixty times greater in amplitude than the electrical activity generated by the brain.

In fetal development the heart forms and starts beating before the brain is developed; this is basic physiology, well known since the 1800's. The heart sends more information to the brain than vice versa through electromagnetic waves. Heart Math research has proven that among the most powerful factors that affect the heart's rhythm are our feelings and emotions. Emotions such as anger, frustration, and anxiety give rise to irregular erratic heart rhythm patterns, depleting our energy and throwing the central nervous system into chaos.

In contrast, positive emotions such as appreciation, joy, and love send a very different signal throughout the body. The heart rhythm pattern becomes highly ordered, looking like a smooth, harmonious wave. This is called a coherent heart rhythm pattern. When we're generating a coherent heart rhythm, the body's systems become synchronized, operating with increased efficiency and harmony.

Even more interesting to me is that the magnetic field produced by the heart is more than 100 times stronger than the field generated by the brain, and it can be detected up to 3 feet away from the body using magnetometers. This led neurophysiologists to observe that the heart communicates with the brain in ways that significantly affect how we perceive and react to the world. These invisible magnetic signals the heart generates have the capacity to affect individuals around us. I spot a photo in a health magazine that sends electricity up my spine. It's almost exactly what I saw in the web. I mentally process this.

The heart has its own neural network in the body, and that network looks like what I saw in the web. If the heart's signals radiate out from our bodies, does that mean other people can pick up on those signals too? It feels like messages from Molli are physically coming through her heart. What if this type of communication is true not only for Molli and me, but humans in general? Maybe the heart is like a transmitter, and this is how we reach one another without words. Could the human heart be THE clue to how people connect to each other without language?

I find some compelling research conducted in 2012 by UC Davis psychologist Emilio Ferrer, Ph.D., and his team. He took thirty-two couples and sat each one alone in a room hooked up to an EKG machine to measure respiration. He then had them perform three tasks for five minutes each. The first task was doing nothing to establish a baseline; the second was to gaze at each other; and the third, trying to imitate each other without touching or speaking. During each task he discovered the partners' heart rates became synchronized—beat to beat.

He then had each partner keep an "emotional journal" for ninety days. Interestingly, the partners tracked each other's ups and downs. In most cases it was the women who shifted their emotions and heart rates to match those of their male partners, signaling that perhaps women are more empathic. The National Science Foundation supported the research.

These findings seem to support my sense that the heart is where the physical and spiritual blend together—where our intuition comes from. If Molli is trying to say something, then I am listening.

An avalanche came rushing into my mind, quickly weaving hypotheses together.

So, the heart really is a transmitter using invisible electromagnetic waves like a radio to communicate feelings and emotions. The brain is hardwired like a landline, but the heart is wireless like a radio. Radio waves, invisible electromagnetic waves, feelings, and emotions all affect heart rhythms. The heart sends signals to the brain that regulate health and behavior—these transmissions are like music!

All these years I had been puzzled by how Maria still gets excited when she hears music that she heard repeatedly at age two. In Rett Syndrome girls, the MECP2 gene responsible for making the protein essential for normal nerve cell function in the brain stops expressing at approximately twenty-four months. The brain is unable to complete the wiring process, slowing further development and impeding the ability to retain memory.

In 1999, the Dixie Chicks (now just called "the Chicks") were wildly popular when their first album *Fly* hit the airwaves. Maria's caregiver at the time was a huge fan, and played that album constantly. To this day, whenever Maria is in pain or I need to brighten her mood, all I have to do is play that music and her disposition becomes positive. How can this be if her brain has not finished wiring? I research how and where the brain stores music and come across research conducted by scientists at the Department of Neurology at the Virchow campus in Berlin, Germany.

They examined a man who lost all of his memories but retained his ability to learn and remember songs. The patient was a sixty-eight-year-old professional cellist who developed encephalitis. The inflammation caused him to develop amnesia so severe that he couldn't remember his professional or personal past (retrograde amnesia), family or friends, or acquire new information (ante retrograde amnesia). Despite this condition his musical memory remained intact. Furthermore, the patient was still able to sight-read and play the cello.

Dr. Ploner developed several tests that took the patient's amnesia into account. Compared to both amateur musicians and professionals from the Berlin Philharmonic, the patient's musical memory was normal. What's more, he displayed not only the ability to remember musical pieces from his past, but also the ability to remember musical pieces that he had never heard before the tests. Carsten Finke, neuroscientist from the University of Berlin, told *Science Daily* that "[the] findings show that musical memory is organized at least partially independent of the hippocampus, a brain structure that is central to memory formation. It is possible that the enormous significance of music throughout all times and in all cultures contributed to the development of an independent memory for music."

I sense that the emotions associated with music are not only located in the brain, but in the heart as well. It just has to be vibrational as well as chemical and neurological. Music may also provide a chilling clue about what might have contributed to Molli's decision that fatal day. The CD in her car sends me on a path to research how music affects the heart. The thought of a song that glorifies suicide is so haunting to me that I cannot let it go.

The scientists in Berlin have proven that music is emotional, primal, and spiritual. If music has great power to call to our highest selves then it can have the opposite power too. I come upon the work of Peter Slight, M.D., a retired Oxford University researcher who studied the effect of music on cardiac rhythms. He discovered that blood pressure and heart rate rise and fall to match the volume and pace of music.

Other research has revealed that musical phrases, chants, or recited prayers that hit a ten-beat rhythm seem to sync with what is called the Meyer wave, which is the natural ebb and flow of heart rate and blood pressure. I always wondered why music was so powerful, and, in many ways, also a universal language that connects us all—just like the web. Dr. Sleight ends his article on this note: "Ironically, the 'Ave Maria' composed by Franz Schubert in 1825, hits this ten-beat rhythm perfectly."

My curiosity about the heart intensified after these discoveries. Innately I have known the heart was more than just a simple pump, but never considered the central role it played throughout human history. I found an article by Mimi Guarneri, M.D, an integrative cardiologist, who states her belief about the heart. She sent my thinking in a new direction.

"There's a physical heart and there's an emotional heart, which responds to the world around you. There's also a spiritual heart, which I believe is where the seat of the soul is located, holding the truth about why you came into this world and what you came here to do as a human being."

Of course! Molli, I want to know the truth about why you came into this world and what you came here to do as a human being. I want to know this about Maria, about myself, about all of us. We come into the world with that knowledge, filled with love and light, but somehow we lose our identity along the way. We get distracted by the vicissitudes of life and cover ourselves with addictions to deal with the suffering; we anesthetize to numb the pain, but that just leads us into the darkness— it dims our light.

IDENTITY CRISIS

*"Your whole idea about yourself is borrowed—borrowed from those
who have no idea of who they are themselves."*

–Osho

I picked up the phone and called Natalie. If anyone could
help me understand what led Molli into the darkness it was
her. Best friends confide in each other more than in their parents, because friends can relate to what each is going through. I
also had the sense that Natalie could speak for her generation.
It's a generation foreign to me—stolen away by Rett Syndrome.
I picked up the phone.

"Hello, Natalie… it's Rob. I think Jay already told you, I'm
the guy who has Molli's heart." All I heard were sobs, sniffles,
then silence. "I'm sorry if this is a bad time…"

"Oh my God..." Natalie hyperventilated in between tears. She struggled to get words out. "I know who you are. I just can't believe I finally... thank you for calling me. Molli—she's alive in you, and I... sorry, I'm not making sense."

"I understand," I told her. "Take your time. I'll stay on the phone with you for as long as it takes... or I can call you back."

"No! I want to hear you," she said. "I want to talk with you. These past two years have been so hard... I just need to know she's okay. So many things have happened... I've been trying to figure out what went wrong. It feels like yesterday and the pain never went away. Maybe I can have some peace hearing her, I mean, you. I mean, there's so much–"

"Slow down," I told her, "take your time. We can talk for as long as you like. I'm sure we both have lots of questions. How about we get to know each other a little bit first, then we can talk about Molli?"

"Good idea," she said, catching her breath as we began a conversation about ourselves, our families, and our lives. But our dialogue soon returned to Molli. I sensed that Natalie was anxious to share everything she knew about her best friend, to try piecing together the puzzle.

Intuition told me to ask questions. I felt Molli's heart beating, and I sensed *Natalie is going to tell you what you need to hear.* My mind told me to wait, that it was a mistake to ask bold questions too soon. *You might push Natalie over the edge—she's too fragile right now.* I decided to listen to Molli's heart.

"Tell me, Natalie, how does such a beautiful person filled with love and light get lost? It seems to me she saw beauty in all things—animals, nature, art. She was even able to see beyond the disabilities of children with special needs and feel their humanity. What the heck happened?"

Natalie composed herself and released the pent-up emotions that have haunted her.

"In my opinion there was a hidden pain inside her," she explained, "but instead of facing it she escaped into the unreal world of social media, which only made the pain worse. I know, because I've been there. She never really shared what the pain was, but I sensed she felt empty inside. I saw her searching for love and acceptance."

"I don't get it. The unreal world of social media? Maria has never experienced these things, and I've never had time for it. How can someone with over 3,000 friends on Facebook not feel accepted?"

"You don't have a Facebook page, do you?" she chuckled.

"Nope."

"Do you use some of the social media apps, like Snapchat or Instagram?"

"Not sure what those are, but I do text," I said. She laughed, and I joked, "I know I'm really advanced... so tell me how this made things worse for her."

"It started in high school with online bullying," she explained. "Come to think of it, that's when she started cutting herself. Molli was a bit of a goofball, but it was all innocent, silly things. Like, we would dress up in these ridiculous outfits and run around Walmart on summer nights. We had a blast."

I remember Jay telling me that Molli started cutting around age fifteen, which is when the darkness came. I decided to ask Natalie about it.

"I don't know what cutting is," I said, "but I do understand bullying. I was different in high school too. I wasn't a jock or very popular. I was quiet, and it came with a price."

"Okay, then you'll get this." Natalie became the teacher. "Let me start with how social media sucks you in and can become addicting. So, for example, you post an honest picture of yourself on Facebook, like Molli dressed up in a wacky outfit having fun, and the next thing you know all these negative and cruel remarks are getting posted and you don't even know who these people are. At least when you were getting bullied you knew who was doing it, right?"

"Yeah, and I could confront that person," I added.

"Right! Now imagine if you couldn't defend yourself, and what's worse, you start to get paranoid thinking like, well maybe my own friends feel that way about me. It's like, you get punished for being yourself online. It's so much harder for girls in high school, you know? We're supposed to be pretty and skinny... these feelings of worthlessness set in and you become even more desperate for acceptance."

"Wait, you're losing me here. How can you not feel accepted when you have over 3,000 friends?"

"They're not really friends," she said. "I mean, some are, but most of them are people you might have something in common with or that you envy and want to be like. So you start sending out friend requests. The more people 'like' you, the more accepted you feel. It feeds on itself. You crave it. You can't grasp that it's fake, and that's when it betrays you."

"How so?"

"For example, you send out a friend request and they don't accept it, so you feel rejected. Next thing you know, self-doubt and anxiety set in. You think, W*hat's wrong with me, I'm not pretty enough, I'm not smart enough? They won't be my friend because of this or that.* You pick yourself apart, looking for things that aren't even true. Then you start comparing yourself to others—that's when you really get in trouble."

"You mean you look at other people's lives wondering why you can't be like them?"

"That's part of it," she said, "but it gets more complicated. People only post the best parts of their lives. You see them on vacation, living in a beautiful house, or getting engaged to the perfect person, so you strive for this perfect life. You try and conform, losing your own identity in the process. I fell into that trap for a while when I first got out of high school. Instead of setting my own goals, I based my life on what others were doing in that fabricated world where you're always comparing yourself."

"That's crazy, Natalie. Can't people see it's like some fake, unreal reality show?"

"Nope. That's why I said it becomes an addiction. It draws you in and you start to believe the lies. When you're back in the real world you see that you're not that perfect person, so you retreat back into the online world and live your life vicariously. That's how you escape the fear."

"Fear of what?"

"Fear of not being perfect. Fear of being rejected. Fear of not being loved. When you live in fear of not being loved, you're in so much pain you go numb. You become emotionally detached from other people to protect yourself. Cutting is all about wanting to *feel something.* You so desperately want to feel something that you cut yourself."

"I understand wanting to feel something, but why would you want to hurt yourself and cause more pain when–"

"Because cutting allows you to be *in control of your pain,*"she told me. "For the first time in your life you can control how deep you cut, where you cut, and how long the cut is going to be. You need the *physical* pain to control *all the pain.*"

There was a long pause. I knew she needed to get this out, so I waited in silence and mulled it over. I understand better now. Something happened to Molli that caused this hidden pain. She got sucked into the social media vortex when she was about fifteen, and she started cutting when faced with her real-world pain.

"Honestly, for the first year after her suicide I was in counseling trying to figure out a lot of stuff," Natalie said. "My therapist helped me understand what was behind the cutting. For some it's about controlling pain. For others it's a release of pain. Looking back, I should have caught it. I feel so guilty…"

She broke down. It hurt me to see her hurting...

"Let's talk about something else," I blurted out, "like..."

She drew in a deep breath to regain her composure.

"No, I want you to hear this. Molli wants you to hear this."

Her words made the hairs on my arms prickle. I too sensed that Molli wanted me to hear this.

"Cutting and suicide are rampant in my generation," she said.

My mind flashed to the dream I had after meeting Jay—All those ghostly girls on the edge of the forest, emerging from the darkness, reaching out to me in silence. Their eyes all looked the same—dull, lightless, and without affect. I kept looking at their cuts and begging, "What are you trying to tell me?"

"It's like we're more connected because of the internet, but more isolated than ever," she continued. "I'm not saying it's the cause of all the problems in my generation, but it seems to be making things worse."

Almost simultaneously we both let out a long sigh...

"Whew. Natalie... heavy. Thank you. You've given me so much. Like you, I'm struggling to piece this together. I feel like Molli is trying to tell us something. She never got a chance to become what she was created to be, to fulfill her purpose, to finish what she came into the world to do as a human being. I know this sounds crazy but–"

"I totally get it," she said. "That's why I'm willing to talk with you. We can help each other. We can talk again before you come up for her celebration of life in June. I'm willing to share this dark stuff because maybe Molli can still make a difference for someone else. I want people to know the damage that suicide leaves behind, and how it throws everyone's life off track."

Natalie's voice crackled, so I changed the subject again. We'd have plenty of time to talk later. Natalie opened my eyes to a world I didn't even know existed. If I was to understand, I needed to know more, so I went on another research quest. The first thing I needed to figure out was how could social media possibly lead to suicide?

I came across a study published in the JAMA Open Network led by Donna Ruch, a research scientist at the Nationwide Children's Hospital who analyzed adolescent suicide trends between 1975 and 2016. Since 2007 the rate of female youth suicides has surged 12.7 percent, prompting researchers to ask questions about the role of social media in adolescent health.

An opinion piece in JAMA Open Network by Joan Luby and Sara Kertz of Southern Illinois University stated, "The fact that social media has become a primary forum for interpersonal engagement in adolescence, a developmental period when social contact is rapidly rising and becoming increasingly important to wellbeing, makes this an area of great potential influence and importance." They also pointed out that more than ninety-five percent of youth are now connected to the internet in some form. They state that girls' use of social media could be "more likely to result in interpersonal stress," a factor implicated in youth suicide. The pair observed that girls use social media more frequently than boys, and are more likely to face cyberbullying.

In another study, Victor Schwartz, chief medical officer at suicide prevention nonprofit The Jed Foundation writes, "For adolescents, using social media in a way that detracts from face-to-face interactions could be particularly detrimental to mental health."

I thought about that day in late November 2016 when my colleague stopped by my apartment in Chicago and took me to lunch. I was observing the family of four sitting across the table from us and none of them were looking at one another. It seemed everyone in the restaurant displayed the addictive behavior of junkies anesthetized with their fix. I remember thinking,

Where are the beautiful human beings I saw in the Ethereal that were filled with light? This feels like a movie where the dystopian future has arrived, or maybe it's an unreal reality show where everything is staged. We are all here craving human touch but are still alone

*sitting across from one another. Does this room represent a dim part
of the web I saw in the Ethereal?*

I researched the root cause of addiction to social media and
smartphone platforms. According to a new study by Harvard
University, the phenomenon of social media addiction can
largely be attributed to the dopamine hits that social network-
ing sites provide. To keep consumers using their products and
services, these platforms produce the same neural circuitry
caused by gambling and recreational drugs. The stream of
tweets, likes, and shares affect the brain's reward area, which
triggers the same kind of chemical reaction as other drugs.
Neuroscientists have compared social media interaction to a
syringe of dopamine injected straight into the nervous system.
When the brain receives a reward, it rewires itself and associates
the drug or activity with positive reinforcement.

Now I understood the power of social media deception. I
also read an article that quoted Chamath Palihapitiya, former
vice president of user growth at Facebook. He told an audience
of Stanford students that he felt "tremendous guilt" for his
involvement in exploiting consumer behavior. "The short-term,
dopamine-driven feedback loops that we have created," he said,
"are destroying how society works."

Research shows that adolescents who habitually use social
media from a young age have severely stunted social interaction skills. Despite the fact that users interact with one another
on these platforms, many of the social skills don't translate to
the real world. Social media provides continuous rewards that
young people don't receive in real life, which causes them
to engage more and more with social media activities. This

eventually leads to interpersonal problems, such as ignoring real-world relationships and real-life physical health.

I was reminded of how tobacco companies purposely designed cigarettes to make tobacco smoke smoother, less harsh, and more appealing to new users, particularly adolescents. No wonder this generation is under so much stress—they're being programmed for addiction.

I thought about what Natalie told me, how the overuse of social media became an addiction and almost caused her to lose her own identity—how she lost her own will to set goals for herself. It reminded me of the elderly Chinese woman in 2016 at the Chinese Bible Church of Oak Park. What she said to me then has a much deeper meaning to me now: "God represents freedom..." and "You can't build a human being in a factory."

When we lose our ability to choose, we lose our freedom and we turn into robots.

That conversation is what prompted me to finish Eknath Easwaran's book, *Conquest of Mind*, and write this in my journal:

Only when choosing in freedom does the human being truly come to life.

Choosing is the opposite of slavery to addiction. Human beings are most alive when God's love and light flourish within us. I understood that love could not exist without free will. But now I see its meaning even clearer. When we succumb to any form of addiction our free will gets ensnared, leading us into the darkness and dimming our light. When I first saw the dark

ONCE WE FORGET WHO WE ARE, OUR LIGHT GOES DIM—WE DON'T FULFILL OUR PURPOSE.

parts of the web, I thought that maybe those were places of hatred, violence, and hopelessness. Now I understand that something sneaky and insidious is at work. Once we forget who we are, our light goes dim—we don't fulfill our purpose.

I read something called the *Global Risks Report 2019,* published by the World Economic Forum, and it caught my attention in a big way. What struck me was that global insurance companies are studying these trends, and they are worried. They noted that, while technological change always causes stress, the fourth industrial revolution is blurring the lines between the human and the technological. We live in a time when physical, digital, and biological worlds are increasingly merged. The result is an increase in loneliness, rising polarization, and a corresponding decline in empathy.

John Scott, head of sustainability risk at Zurich Insurance Group states, "Emotionally, people are quite lonely. We're seeing in many societies a kind of breakdown of family, or connection with family... I think it's also a demographic thing; younger people are more tuned into using technology and social media, and to live in a world talking to machines through chatbots. That can create all sorts of emotions of fear and frustration, and in some cases that frustration can get expressed as anger." The report noted that we are entering an "age of anger," and this posed a significant threat to worldwide stability.

I remember what Natalie once told me: "I'm willing to share this *dark stuff* because maybe Molli can still make a difference for someone else." When I was in the Ethereal, I understood that I was bound to all of creation by the web. I knew that if I hurt myself, I hurt everything connected to me, but if I loved then the light would spread. *Is this part of what you want to do now, Molli, to help the light spread, and keep others from falling into the darkness?*

Several weeks passed as I processed my research and I realized that a spiritual partnership was born the day that part of Molli was put inside me. I remember how I felt when I awoke from my four-day coma, after I flatlined in January of 2016. The physical pain could not compare to the spiritual pain of not having found and fulfilled my purpose at age fifty-six. I can't imagine the pain of not having fulfilled one's purpose at age twenty.

Sitting at my desk, I have what felt like another conversation with Molli: "*Remember what I told you that day I met your dad? I said, 'We're in this together and we'll figure it out.' I feel like we can help each other fulfill our dual purposes, but you need to tell me the rest of your story… okay? Let's call Natalie.*"

I called Natalie and we picked up right where we left off the last time, almost as if we never stopped talking.

"Like I was telling you, that first year after her suicide I went through a rough patch," she said. "I felt so guilty. I tried to understand why she did it, so I began to research suicide online and I saw terrible things. That opened up a realm of darkness in my mind, and one depressing thought led to another. It was all I could think about—the same stuff that took Molli almost took hold of me!"

I asked her what "terrible things" she meant.

"The dark web is where the internet trolls live," she explained. "They wait in the shadows and prey on your fears. That's how they spread disinformation and hate. It's like, if you're struggling with depression or something, they can actually coax you into killing yourself or someone else. Before you know it, you start to believe the lies."

The last time the hairs on the back of my neck stood up like this was when I met the pastor on that flight from Los Angeles to Seattle.

Night after night he would go into the woods casting a shadow of his own image in the darkness. He told me how dark forces identify our fears, attach to those fears, then attack in our weakest moment. He believed the lies too, until the darkness used him up and betrayed him.

"What lies?"

"You know, like 'everyone would be better off without me,' or 'what's the use of living with all this pain?' Molli's pain didn't go away, it just got transferred to me and everyone else. I didn't realize it at the time, but at age twenty I was at a formative place in my life, deciding if I wanted to just work or pursue college. I got lost for a while because I used the sadness and guilt to cover up my own flaws. That's how my life got thrown off track for a year. That's what I want people to know, the damage that's left behind... nothing good comes from suicide."

I think of my brother-in-law, Frosty. His life was cut short by suicide three years ago and the collateral damage, especially to his parents, continues taking its toll. Their health has rapidly declined, accelerating the aging process caused by a lingering pain that cannot be soothed. I also sensed Frosty's deep regret of the pain transferred to his daughter. It helped when I returned from my coma and delivered the message that he was okay, but I also learned on the other side that he ached with the knowledge of their suffering.

Natalie breathed a sigh of relief—she finally let it all out, and I sensed a shift in her tone of voice. I remained silent as she continued.

"But this year, I'm more excited than ever about our celebration of life gathering, because now I have hope that Molli's life carries on and has meaning through you."

I told her that the feeling was mutual, and I couldn't wait until we met in person.

"How's this for being tech-savvy," I told her, "you don't even have to email me the address of the park where you have the gathering. Just text the name and I'll meet everyone there."

"Wow, you really *are* advanced," she said, as we shared a laugh. "See you then."

The next day, Susan from Gift of Hope followed up with a courtesy call to see how my meeting with Jay unfolded. I explained what transpired and Susan sounded awestruck.

"Rob, this story is profound," she said, then followed up with a request. She wanted to share my experience with their donor family services department to help promote organ donation. She said if Jay and I approve, she'd bring a photographer to Molli's celebration of life, and she'd write up a short story.

"What do you think?" she asked me.

I thought about Molli, and her heart raced inside me. All at once I felt a rush of the same oneness I felt in the Ethereal, the state where I realized that everything in the universe is one. I am not my body, race, or religion. I experienced unity, a single human race all made of the same substance. It's as though I felt Molli trying to say that when she chose to donate her organs she meant it as a gift. It felt like the ultimate expression of oneness.

I remember what Jay told me in the restaurant. He didn't even know she was an organ donor. "But in the end, she gave away everything, man. Who knows how many lives she saved?"

I told Susan I loved her idea, let's do it. I couldn't think of a better way to honor Molli's memory.

"Great," she said. "I won't have any trouble getting Jay's permission when I tell him about the device I'm bringing."

"Device?" I asked her.

"It's a stethoscope hooked up to an iPad," she said. "Everyone will not only hear Molli's heart, but will actually be able to see the wavelengths, kind of like an EKG."

"That's incredible technology," I told her. "Did I mention that the heart pump that kept me alive until I got Molli's heart was also controlled by an iPad? I wouldn't have made it without that device."

We thanked God for Apple and shared a laugh, both knowing that it would be a remarkable blessing for Molli's friends and family who were still struggling with their loss."

June 9, 2019 I flew to Chicago to attend the event. When I arrived at the park I scouted around for the right picnic shelter. I spotted a young woman with bright pink hair among the crowd, and Molli's heart involuntarily pounded when I saw her. I remembered my research on how the heart transmits feelings and emotions using invisible electromagnetic waves. Message sent, message received—it was Natalie.

We spotted each other and made beelines to meet in the middle of the parking lot and embrace.

Neither of us could hold back our tears. We needed no words.

Three other girls approached for a hug and Natalie broke the silence with a chuckle.

"You have officially met the girl squad," she told me. "We're the ones that dressed up in crazy outfits and ran around Walmart with Molli on summer nights."

Natalie took me by the hand and led me to the picnic table where more friends and family were gathered.

"Come on," she said, "let me introduce you..."

Friends approached one-by-one, and after I'd met them all Natalie hefted a large book onto the picnic table in front of me.

"I have a surprise."

It was a beautifully arranged scrapbook filled with scenes from Molli's life. I was flabbergasted by the care and creativity that went into this tribute and could only imagine how many painstaking hours she'd devoted to it. As I turned each page, Natalie and friends filled in details.

One page, however, needed no explanation. The inscription read, "Thank you, Rob, for giving me a form of life again." It should have felt strange to read the words "thank you" to me, because I fully understood that I owed everything to Molli. Nevertheless, I sensed warmth radiating from her heart. It's understood that we both honor the partnership—helping each other fulfill our purpose.

Susan was with the photographer just outside our radius, snapping pictures while taking care not to intrude on the day's magic. When she sensed an opening, she called us over.

"Who wants to hear Molli's heart beating inside Rob?"

A silence fell among the crowd, and everyone seemed frozen in place. Many started to cry, others smiled, and one woman slowly raised her hand in the air. Susan suggested that I sit in my car so we could better hear the heartbeat, and a line quickly formed in the parking lot.

The photographer positioned herself outside the car's front passenger window to give us privacy. Susan placed the stethoscope on my chest, and the iPad rested on my leg. I noticed Jay was the first one in line. He had a tentative look that reminded me of the first day we met. I could feel Molli's heart quivering.

Jay stared at me as he inserted the earbuds connected to the stethoscope. With each heartbeat his smile reacted in tandem, becoming wider until all his teeth were in full view.

He looked down at the iPad, watching the wavelengths of Molli's heartbeat, then back at me.

"I'm glad you didn't give up on finding us," he said.

Natalie anxiously awaited her turn. Her eyes were glassy and she had one hand over her mouth to contain her emotions. To think that she could hear her best friend's heartbeat again was overwhelming. She dared not look at me; that would have sent her over the edge. Instead she kept her eyes fixed on the iPad and inserted the earbuds.

In anticipation of a total breakdown, silently I spoke to Molli: "*Let's just stay calm, we'll get through this...*" Instead, something wonderful and unexpected happened. Natalie had a dreamy look, as if she was recalling only the best of times she and Molli spent together. I felt enveloped in a blanket of peace. Whatever troubles and darkness ensnared Molli's young life, and however her loved ones have suffered, it dissipated in that moment.

Gazing out toward the park, Natalie removed the earbuds with a knowing smile.

"If Molli were here," she declared, "she'd be turning cartwheels in the grass."

Molli's heart was at rest. Together we'd continue our journey on earth, until I see her again in the Ethereal, perfect and whole, just like I saw Maria—her eyes filled with light.

QUARKS OF LIGHT

"We can easily forgive a child who is afraid of the dark; the real tragedy of life is when men are afraid of the light."

–Plato

L ooking back on these last years that began with my heart attack on January 26, 2016, I think about what I have come to understand.

While writing this book, I've kept a small glass urn on my desk. It contains the ash remains of my brother-in-law, Frosty. When I flatlined, it was Frosty who came to me in spirit and said *"Tell my family I'm in a good place."* He provided the first clue of what I would come to learn through researching the basic tenets of the world's religions. Everything we have shall pass away—but spirit remains eternal.

> EVERYTHING WE HAVE SHALL PASS AWAY—BUT SPIRIT REMAINS ETERNAL.

Gazing upon this urn reminds me that all our fears, doubts, and pain will eventually end up in a pile of ashes. What we consume, the clothes we wear, the cars we drive, the house we live in are folly compared to how we allow the Divine to express through us. Every human being has the potential to become what God created us to be. We can choose to love, spreading the light within, illuminating the path for others; or become ensnared by the darkness, moving us further away from God's irreproachable light.

I now believe that when all the outward trappings of our physical bodies are stripped down to our essence, every living being is made of light. Ancient religious scriptures throughout human history have associated light with divine consciousness and intelligence, from which everything originated. Science is now proving that *light* is the cornerstone of physics and natural law.

Scientists specializing in quantum physics make the case that we are all made of the same cosmic material, and that our brains trick us into believing we are separate. All matter is made of atoms. Atoms have a nucleus that contains protons, neutrons, and electrons. These particles in turn are made of quarks, the smallest building blocks of matter. Broken down to the subatomic level, they are made of pure light. These quarks combine and have a variety of intrinsic properties that create infinite possibilities in the universe—the unique combinations determine whether something is going to be a tree or a person.

To think that quarks of light could be the fundamental essence of all creation makes me wonder—are we conceived through light? Researchers at Northwestern University in Chicago made a stunning discovery in April of 2016. A radiant burst of light, known as a zinc spark, occurs when a human egg is fertilized. It was also discovered, the size of these "sparks" is a direct measure of the quality of the egg and its ability to develop into an embryo. Teresa Woodruff, one of the study's two senior authors and an expert in ovarian biology said, "We discovered the zinc spark just five years ago in the mouse, and to see the zinc radiate out in a burst from each human egg was breathtaking."

Be it a human embryo, a plant, or the entire universe—all of creation begins with a spark of light. Scientific studies are also building explanations of how we are all connected through a phenomenon known as quantum entanglement. The theory states that when two atoms come into contact with each other, whatever happens to one of the atoms can instantly affect the other, even if the particles are separated.

> BE IT A HUMAN EMBRYO, A PLANT, OR THE ENTIRE UNIVERSE—ALL OF CREATION BEGINS WITH A SPARK OF LIGHT.

I am beginning to see how these studies relate to one of the insights revealed to me in the Ethereal. While I was in that place, I remember thinking, *Of course! How simple. It has to be designed this way. Everything is created from the same ingredients, the same formula. All people, all creatures, everything animate and inanimate are all connected. We just manifest physical forms differently, but all things are one. This is the only way the Creator could have designed it. Only humans have made it so complicated.*

In the Ethereal I understood that I was part of the interactive web made of twinkling lights that stretched into infinity, and I realized that each quark of light represented a life and there was no place to hide my actions in the universe, whether good or bad. The dark parts of the web had confounded me, but now I understand that these are places where humans are not emanating light. The web as a whole represents the epic light and dark struggles for all of humanity in every age. Darkness comes in many shapes and forms, but has only one goal: to ultimately snuff out our light.

A chilling example of darkness comes to mind as I recall the conversation with Dr. Uriel, when he told me he got approval to transplant me even though I had prostate cancer. I listened to him tell the story of how his mother watched half her family murdered by the Nazis in what was called *selection process,* determining on the spot by the standards *they* set who had enough *value* to live or die. It left an indelible mark on my spirit.

He told me that morning, "I promised myself that when I became a doctor, I would never practice medicine that way. Because everyone has value, everyone has the right to live." That comment prompted me to research how the Nazi darkness almost spread throughout the world. I wanted to find the root cause, the source of such madness that could drive one race to dehumanize another. I was not surprised to discover that it began with a belief that God was dead.

Long before Adolf Hitler wrote *Mein Kampf* (My Fight) in 1923, which promoted the central ideas behind Nazism, his thoughts were influenced by the nineteenth century German philosopher and atheist Friedrich Nietzsche, who proclaimed in his writings that the "death of God" would ultimately be a *good* thing for society.

Nietzsche promulgated the idea that the "superhuman" being must create his or her own identity through self-realization, without relying on anything transcending that life, such as God or a soul. Hitler made very selective use of Nietzsche's philosophy, distorting many of his concepts to poison the minds of his followers. When he came to power he created his own set of values within the moral vacuum of nihilism to justify the systematic killing of six million Jews and ultimate decimation of his own country.

Hitler used the concepts of "God is dead" and the creation of a "superhuman" race. Dictators around the world emerged from the shadows—using darkness to gather power unto themselves—by attempting to snuff out the light of their own people. More than eighty-five million people perished during World War II, which was approximately three percent of the entire world population in 1940.

I believe the greatest experiment of evil and darkness ultimately failed because dehumanization was at the core of the Nazi strategy, and you cannot separate God from the human— we are one. They tried to force God out of the human through propaganda, fear, and every imaginable form of diabolical torture. They did their worst deeds under the shroud of secrecy, but what they didn't know was that there is no place to hide one's actions, good or bad, in the universe.

Although a study of Nazi terror is horrifying in scale, I have come to understand that we each experience a mini struggle of dark and light on a daily basis. We make choices every day out of free will to spread the light or hide in the darkness. We were designed by the Creator with the innate ability to recognize the difference between good and evil. I believe God wove the universal fabric of the web into us as our moral compass. Darkness creeps into our lives when we disconnect

> DARKNESS CREEPS INTO OUR LIVES WHEN WE DISCONNECT OURSELVES FROM GOD'S LOVE AND LIGHT.

ourselves from God's love and light. The next thing we know, we are overcome with anxiety and we forget our real identity— our purpose remains unfulfilled.

As the human race enters the fourth industrial revolution, described by the *Global Risks Report 2019*, I see a new iteration of darkness spreading throughout the world. The blend between the human and technological has the potential to create a soulless society. This seems frighteningly familiar. Anger, anxiety, and fear are on the rise, while some trends show a decline of human empathy and compassion. This can spiral into self-dehumanization. When we see ourselves as unworthy, the darkness overwhelms us.

There is only one way to keep the darkness from spreading: to understand that we are made of light and that we are all connected. The nature of the universe is unity; our destinies are inextricably woven together by the web. The web in the Ethereal is a reflection of the choices we make on Earth. The hope of peace for the world and peace within ourselves can only take place when we realize that our actions in the temporal world have a direct impact on everything else. While in the web I experienced this: *If I hurt myself, I hurt everything connected to me. But if I love, the light will spread.*

When I saw Maria in the Ethereal she was perfect and whole—her eyes filled with light. Not the kind of light we see in the natural world, but the spirit of light that animates all life. When I asked her how I could help her in the temporal world, she only spoke three words: *Just love me.* Love is the universal language God uses to speak through all of creation. Light is the energy source God uses to create. Light expels darkness, heals us, and transforms us.

These experiences showed me that God and love and light are all one. Maria has been the shining embodiment of that pure, untarnished love in my life. She is the one who showed me what matters, helping me to understand that the way we bring more love into the world is by using our free will to act. Many times these actions come in the form of unglamorous

> LOVE IS THE UNIVERSAL LANGUAGE GOD USES TO SPEAK THROUGH ALL OF CREATION. LIGHT IS THE ENERGY SOURCE GOD USES TO CREATE. LIGHT EXPELS DARKNESS, HEALS US, AND TRANSFORMS US.

moments, when we simply use our hands to serve another.

Then when my own body broke down, I experienced the love of others who used their free will to serve me. Now my mind returns to the first moment I experienced the light in my crib. The glowing orb descended on me and I wondered, what is "it?" Does every child have one, too? I now know that everyone does—only I was blessed to remember it. Then, all those decades later, I was given another glimpse into the spiritual realm to remind me of this truth: the light of God is our real identity.

I saw for myself that what awaits us on the other side is the light. Yet I also now know that we do not have to wait, nor do we have to look outside ourselves. It is already there, for the light is within each of us.

REVIEW INQUIRY

Hey, it's Rob here.

I hope you've enjoyed the book, finding it both inspirational and useful. I have a favor to ask you.

Would you consider giving it a rating wherever you bought the book? Online book stores are more likely to promote a book when they feel good about its content, and reader reviews are a great barometer for a book's quality.

So please go to the website of wherever you bought the book, search for my name and the book title, and leave a review. If able, perhaps consider adding a picture of you holding the book. That increases the likelihood your review will be accepted!

Many thanks in advance,
Rob A. Gentile

WILL YOU SHARE THE LOVE?

Get this book for a friend, associate, or family member!

If you have found this book valuable and know others who would find it useful, consider buying them a copy as a gift. Special bulk discounts are available if you would like your whole team or organization to benefit from reading this. Just visit https://robagentile.com/contact/

WOULD YOU LIKE ROB TO SPEAK TO YOUR ORGANIZATION?

Book Rob Now!

Rob A. Gentile accepts a limited number of speaking engagements each year. To learn how you can bring his message to your organization, visit https://robagentile.com/contact/

ABOUT THE AUTHOR

 Rob A. Gentile is the son of Italian immigrants. He grew up in Aliquippa, Pennsylvania, where his father worked in a steel mill. Gentile has spent his career as a sales representative in the steel industry while married to his wife Melanie for over thirty years.

Together they have devoted themselves to their daughter with special needs, Maria, who is in her twenties. Throughout her childhood he grappled with difficult questions about prayer and why children must suffer. Answers came in a sudden and unexpected way—at age fifty-six he had a massive heart attack, then flatlined, and had a near-death experience.

His self-discovery and spiritual awakening continued while waiting to receive a donor heart. *Quarks of Light* is his first book.

Rob can be reached at: https://robagentile.com/contact/

Made in United States
North Haven, CT
31 May 2022

19689752R00146